DURHAM,
NORTH PENNINES
AND TYNE & WEAR

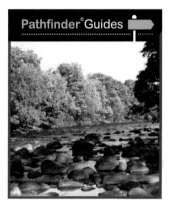

Pathfinder®Guides

Outstanding
Circular Walks

Originally compiled by
Brian Conduit and John Brooks
Revised by Neil Coates

Text:	Brian Conduit, John Brooks
	Revised text for the 2008 and 2017 editions, Neil Coates
Photography:	Brian Conduit, John Brooks, Neil Coates.
	Front cover: Neil Coates
Editorial:	Ark Creative (UK) Ltd
Design:	Ark Creative (UK) Ltd

© Crown copyright / Ordnance Survey Limited, 2017
Published by Crimson Publishing Ltd under licence from Ordnance Survey Limited.
Pathfinder, Ordnance Survey, OS and the OS logos are registered trademarks of
Ordnance Survey Limited and are used under licence from Ordnance Survey Limited.
Text © Crimson Publishing Limited, 2017

This product includes mapping data licensed from Ordnance Survey
© Crown copyright and database rights (2017) OS 150002047

ISBN 978-0-31909-041-1

While every care has been taken to ensure the accuracy of the route directions, the
publishers cannot accept responsibility for errors or omissions, or for changes in
details given. The countryside is not static: hedges and fences can be removed, stiles
can be replaced by gates, field boundaries can be altered, footpaths can be rerouted
and changes in ownership can result in the closure or diversion of some concessionary
paths. Also, paths that are easy and pleasant for walking in fine conditions may
become slippery, muddy and difficult in wet weather, while stepping stones across
rivers and streams may become impassable.

If you find an inaccuracy in either the text or maps, please write to Crimson
Publishing at the address below.

First published 2000 by Jarrold Publishing. Revised and reprinted 2008, 2010.

This edition first published in Great Britain 2017 by Crimson Publishing.

Crimson Publishing, 19-21C Charles Street, Bath, BA1 1HX

www.pathfinderwalks.co.uk

Printed in India by Replika Press Pvt. Ltd. 4/17

A catalogue record for this book is available from the British Library

Front cover: Smardale Gill and Viaduct
Previous page: The River Tees below Holwick

Contents

Short walks

Walks of modest length, likely to involve some modest uphill walking

More challenging walks which may be longer and/or over more rugged terrain, often with some stiff climbs

Keymap 1

SCALE 1:263 157 or 1 INCH to about 4¼ MILES 1CM to 2.6KM

KILOMETRES

KEYMAP HEIGHTS SHOWN IN METRES

MILES

Milton
Rowfoot
A689
Tindale
Midgeholme
Lambley
Stonehouse
Whitfield
Farlam
Hallbankgate
Tindale Tarn
Hayton
19
How
Talkin
Tindale
Forest Head
Whitfield Moor
Faugh
Castle Carrock
King's Forest
of Geltsdale
511
Slaggyford
A689
Ninebanks
Chim
Whitton
482
River Gelt
Geltsdale Middle
525
Kirkhaugh
Cumrew
458
Ayle
524
A686
Hornsby
Newbiggin
501
657
Raise
Alston
Nenthall
Ainstable
Croglin
810
21
Armathwaite
226
Watch Hill
507
Gilderdale
Forest
Bayles
Middle Fell
8
Ruckcroft
Scale Houses
664
Leadgate
Nenthead
Staffield
258
Renwick
580
ALSTON MOOR
614
High Bankhill
A686
Garrigill
Kirkoswald
20
673
Lazonby
Gamblesby
Melmerby Fell
Burnhope Seat
746
Glassonby
Melmerby
710
North Dykes
Little Salkeld
Round Hill
685
Great Salkeld
Hunsonby
Cross Fell
893
Salkeld Dykes
Winskill
Ousby
847
Milburn Forest
Viewing Hill
640
Plumpton Head
Langwathby
Skirwith
Townhead
Kirkland
Great Dun Fell
794
Edenhall
Blencarn
Cow Green Reservoir
286
Whins Pond
Culgaith
767
PENRITH
A686
Milburn
Dufton Fell
Countess Pillar
Newbiggin
396
692
A66
Temple Sowerby
Knock
12
Yanwath
Brougham Castle
Kirkby Thore
481
Dufton
Murton Fell
Clifton
Peel Tower
220
Long Marton
26
673
745
Tirril
Melkinthorpe
Cliburn
Brampton
13
ROMAN ROAD
Lowther Hackthorpe
116
Bolton
Crackenthorpe
APPLEBY-IN-WESTMORLAND
Murton
Great Strickland
Morland
King's Meaburn
Colby
Hilton
Whale
Little Strickland
Newby
Appleby Castle
Warcop Fell
Bampton
341
Sleagill
Hoff
23
Great Ormside
Sandford
Bampton Common
Bampton Grange
Rosgill
Reagill
Maulds Meaburn
166
Warcop
172
Helbeck
Shap Abbey
Drybeck
Great Musgrave
Castle
Shap
Crosby Ravensworth
321
Bleatarn
16
Keld
Hardendale
12
Great Asby
Little Musgrave
RAWSWATER RESR
Oddendale
Soulby
A685
Hotel
Ralfland Forest
A6
187
Winton
Wet Sleddale Reservoir
Crosby Ravensworth Fell
Great Asby Scar
14
Crosby Garrett
13
Mardale Common
412
Sunbiggin
Little Asby
Waitby
KIRKBY STE
tescarth Pass
Orton
Raisbeck
5
Smardale
Nateby
Sadgill
530
Shap Fells
Tebay Services
Kelleth
Newbiggin-on-Lune
Ash Fell
A683
Greenholme
River Lune
385
B6259
Bretherdale Head
Tebay
Gaisgill
Cotegill
Bowderdale
Ravenstonedale
16
Lowbridge
Forest Hall
West Fell
Weasdale
Pendragon Castle
Outgill

Riding Mill
Stocksfield
Dalton Juniper
Catton
Slaley
New Ridley
Hedley on the Hill
Chopwell
Blackhall Mill
Whitley Chapel
Healey
Whittonstall
Newlands
Hamster
Ebchester
Allendale Town
•375
Coalpits Grange
Minsteracres
Kiln Pit Hill
Shotleyfield
VINDOMORA
Hexhamshire Common
SLALEY FOREST
Barleyhill
Carterway Heads
Shotley Bridge
Medd
Lea
Broadwell House
Blanchland Moor
447
Derwent Reservoir
CONSETT
Sinderhope
Allendale Common
St Mary's Abbey
Blanchland
410
Edmundbyers
Allensford
Castleside
Knitsley
572
427
Baybridge
Hunstanworth
384
Muggleswick
375
Healeyfield
Rowley
Green Hill
Byerhope Reservoir
Nookton Fell
478
Townfield
Muggleswick Common
12
Hisehope Reservoir
Smiddy Shaw Reservoir
Butterfield
Allenheads
581
Bolt's Law
540
Waskerley 22
Satley
Stangend Currick
Middlehope Moor
603
Rookhope
Stanhope Common
516
Collier Law
Wolsingham Park Moor
Tunstall Reservoir
A689
Lanehead
Cowshill
Wearhead
Westgate 7
Eastgate
Crawleyside
Stanhope
TOW LAW
Burnhope Reservoir
Weardale
1
A689
Frosterley
10
Wolsingham
B6296
Thornley
Ireshopeburn
St John's Chapel
Daddry Shield
Hill End
White Kirkley
20
Ireshope Moor
Three Pikes
Chapelfell Top 696
Westernhope Moor
675
Snowhope Hill
Bollihope Common
St John's Hall
487
Pikeston Fell
Redford
Bedburn
Toll
Langdon Common
18
Langdon Beck
Newbiggin Common
Middleton Common
Pawlaw Pike
HAMSTERLEY FOREST
Toll
Hamster
Forest-in-Teesdale
Ettersgill
•565
Eggleston Common
Woodland
11
Cronkley Fell
High Force
Newbiggin
25
Middleton-in-Teesdale
Woodland Fell
319
Butterknowle
Morley
Holwick
27
B6282
Eggleston
•461
Copley
Cock
NE FOREST
Lune Moor
Bowbank
Mickleton
Burnt Houses
Thringarth
Grassholme Reservoir
Romaldkirk
Kinninvie
Raby Cast
Grains o' th' Beck
River Lune
Grassholme
Kelton
Hunderthwaite
Hury
Cotherstone
Stainton
Staindrop
6
Dow Crag
562
Selset Reservoir
Hury Reservoir
Lartington
11
Stainton Grove
Cleatlam
Little Newsham
Stainmore Common
Balderhead Reservoir
Blackton Reservoir
Clove Lodge
312
24
A67
BARNARD CASTLE
Whorlton
North Stainmore
Cotherstone Moor
439
Startforth
Castle
Eggleston Abbey
Wycliffe
Thorpe
South Stainmore
A66
515
ROMAN ROAD
13
Bowes
Castle
Gilmonby
A67
Boldron
17
Hutton Magna
Ovingl
Ca
Barras
Heggerscales
518
Moudy Mea
28
Brignall
Scargill
221
Smallways
Lane Head West
Layton
STAINMORE FOREST
•446
West Hope
Barningham
East Stang
Barningham Moor
447
Dalton
Gayles
Newsham
ton Fell
Sleightholme Moor
Cleasby Hill
•510
554
Kexwith Moor
Kirby Hill
Whashton
Standards
Tan Hill
Arkengarthdale Moor
Whaw
522
Hurst Moor
Hurst
Ravenseat
West Stonesdale
Stonesdale Moor
668
Rogan's Seat
671
Great Pinseat
583
Langthwaite
Washfold

SCALE 1:263 157 or 1 INCH to about 4¼ MILES *1CM to 2.6KM*

0   2   4   6   8   10   KILOMETRES   15

0   2   4   6   MILES   8   10

KEYMAP HEIGHTS SHOWN IN METRES

Haydon Bridge
Oakwood
Bridge End
Corbridge
Newton
A69
Ovingham
Wylam
B6537
70
HEXHAM
Dilston
Ovington
Castle
Low Gate
Langley Castle
B6305
299
Dalton
Juniper
Slaley
Healey
DERE STREET
Ridley
Hedley on the Hill
Chopwell
Catton
Whitley Chapel
B6309
Whittonstall
Blackhall Mill
New Ebch
Allendale Town
375
SLALEY FOREST
Coalpits Grange
Minsteracres
A68
Kiln Pit Hill
Newlands
VINDOMORA
Shotley Bridge
Hexhamshire Common
Broadwell House
Blanchland Moor
410
Barleyhill
Shotleyfield
CONSETT
Sinderhope
447
St Mary's Abbey
Blanchland
427
Edmundbyers
384
Carterway Heads
B6278
269
Allendale Common
500
Baybridge
Muggleswick
Allensford
Castleside
Knitsley
Rowley
Green Hill
Byerhope Reservoir
Nookton Fell
478
Hunstanworth
Townfield
375
Muggleswick Common
12
Healeyfield
Shield
572
Allenheads
Bolt's Law
561
540
Hisehope Reservoir
Smiddy Shaw Reservoir
Butsfi
Satley
cleugh
T
Stangend Currick
Middlehope Moor
Rookhope
Stanhope Common
Waskerley
Waskerley Reservoir
22
A689
603
Cowshill
Wearhead
7
Westgate
Eastgate
Crawleyside
Stanhope
516
Collier Law
Wolsingham Park Moor
Tunstall Reservoir
TOW LAW
Lanehead
Burnhope Reservoir
Ireshopeburn
Weardale
1
A689
Frosterley
10
Wolsingham
Thornley
B6296
St John's Chapel
Daddry Shield
Hill End
White Kirkley
20
707
Ireshope Moor
Snowhope Hill
Bollihope Common
St John's Hall
Three Pikes
Chapelfell Top
696
Westernhope Moor
675
487
Pawlaw Pike
Pikeston Fell
Redford
Toll
Bedburn
ood
23
Langdon Common
18
Langdon Beck
Newbiggin Common
Middleton Common
Toll
Ham
Widdybank
Ettersgill
565
HAMSTERLEY FOREST
11
Fell
Cauldron Snout
Forest-in-Teesdale
Newbiggin
Eggleston Common
Woodland
319
Butterkno
Cronkley Fell
High Force
25
Middleton-in-Teesdale
Woodland Fell
B6282
18
Copley
Mickle Fell
790
Holwick
27
Bowbank
Eggleston
461
Burnt Houses
LUNE   FOREST
Lune Moor
Mickleton
Startforth
B6279
Ratl
Thringarth
Grassholme Reservoir
Romaldkirk
Kinninvie
Grains o' th' Beck
River Lune
Grassholme
Hunderthwaite
Stainton
ROMAN ROAD
A
Kelton
Setset Reservoir
Hury
Hury Reservoir
Cotherstone
Stainton Grove
11
Cleatlar
Dow Crag
562
Hunderthwaite Moor
Lartington
24
BARNARD CASTLE
Whorl
Stainmore Common
Balderhead Reservoir
Blackton Reservoir
312
Cotherstone Moor
Clove Lodge
Pennine Way
Startforth
Castle
Egglestone Abbey
North Stainmore
Deep Dale
Boldron
4
17
Brough
South Stainmore
515
439
A67
Bowes
ROAD
Brough Sowerby
518
Moudy Mea
A66
13
ROMAN ROAD
Castle
Gilmonby
28
Brignall
Kaber
Barras
Heggerscales
Bowes Moor
446
Scargill
221
85
STAINMORE   FOREST
West Hope
Barningham
Dalton
Rookby
Winton Fell
Sleightholme Moor
Scargill High Moor
The Stang
East Hope
447
Barningham Moor
232
Y STEPHEN
662
Cleasby Hill
510
Tan Hill
554

TYNE
HEBBURN
Monkton
A1300
Cleadon
15
Whitburn
BLAYDON
Byker
Walker
Harton
Marsden Bay
RYTON
Dunston
Pelaw
Fellgate
Boldon Colliery
West Boldon
East Boldon
Fulwell
Roker
WHICKHAM
GATESHEAD
Felling
Wrekenton
A184
A167
A1
A1018
Greenside
Barlow
Metro Centre
Castletown
Southwick
SUN
Rowlands Gill
Gibside
A692
A694
Marley Hill
Sunniside
Angel of the North
Lamesley
Kibblesworth
A194(M)
A1231
South Hylton
A183
Hendon
A1018
Burnopfield
A6076
Washington Services
BIRTLEY
WASHINGTON
3
Fatfield
New Silksworth
A690
Hyhope
Hobson
Tanfield
Ouston
Penshaw
Doxford Park
Dipton
Beamish
A693
Pelton
Shiney Row
New Herrington
A19
Seaton
ANNFIELD PLAIN
STANLEY
Grange Villa
Bournmoor
HOUGHTON-LE-SPRING
A693
South Moor
The Middles
Craghead
CHESTER-LE-STREET
Great Lumley
Fence Houses
HETTON-LE-HOLE
Dalton-le-Dale
Murton
A6076
Maiden Law
Holmside
Waldridge
Plawsworth
Woodstone Village
West Rainton
East Rainton
Cold Hesle
Lanchester
Burnhope
Edmondsley
Kimblesworth
A1(M)
A690
Easington Lane
A19
Hawtho
Langley Park
Witton Gilbert
Pity Me
Finchale Priory
Pittington
Littletown
South Hetton
A182
Easington
Quebec
Esh
Bearpark
Crook Hall
Carville
Sherburn
Sherburn Hill
Haswell
Haswell Plough
Shotton Colliery
PETERL
Cornsay
Ushaw Moor
DURHAM
Shincliffe
Shadforth
Ludworth
Thornley
Shotton
Esh Winning
East Hedleyhope
New Brancepeth
High Shincliffe
A177
A688
A181
Wheatley Hill
Castle Eden
Waterhouses
BRANDON
A690
Brancepeth
A1(M)
Bowburn
Cassop
193
Wingate
Sunniside
Stanley Crook
Oakenshaw
Sunderland Bridge
Croxdale
Durham Services
Quarrington Hill
Deaf Hill
Station Town
Roddymoor
Billy Row
A167
Hett
Kelloe
Trimdon Grange
Trimdon Colliery
WILLINGTON
Byers Green
Tudhoe
Coxhoe
Trimdon
CROOK
Newfield
A688
SPENNYMOOR
Cornforth
Fishburn
Howden-le-Wear
Witton-le-Wear
Hunwick
Ferryhill
A177
High Grange
A689
Middlestone Moor
16
Kirk Merrington
Chilton Lane
Bishop Middleham
Sedgefield
A689
Witton Castle
Escomb
House
Castle
Coundon
Chilton
Witton Park
BISHOP AUCKLAND
Rushyford
A689
Bradbury
Wynyard Village
Etherley
St Helen Auckland
SHILDON
Middridge
Mordon
A177
Thorpe Larches
West Auckland
A6072
NEWTON AYCLIFFE
A167
A1(M)
Foxton
Thorpe Thewles
2
Wolvis
Evenwood
Bildershaw
Redworth
Aycliffe Village
114
Elstob
Stillington
Whitton
Carlton
Norton
6
Bolam
Heighington
Great Stainton
Bishopton
Wackerfield
Hilton
Houghton-le-Side
Brafferton
Coatham Mundeville
Little Stainton
Redmarshall
STOCKTON-ON-TEES
Ingleton
Killerby
Denton
A68
Barmpton
A1027
A135
Gainford
Walworth
A167
Sadberge
Elton
A66
Thorna on-Tees
Piercebridge
High Coniscliffe
A68
Great Burdon
Longnewton
Urlay Nook
Eaglescliffe
Caldwell
Eppleby
Low Coniscliffe
Cleasby
DARLINGTON
Egglescliffe
Aislaby
Ingleby Barwick
Stanwick Camp
Manfield
Aldbrough St John
Stapleton
A66
Hurworth-on-Tees
Low Dinsdale
Durham Tees Valley Airport
Middleton St George
Yarm
A1044
East Layton
Stanwick-St-John
A66(M)
Neasham
Low Worsall
Kirklevington
A66
Melsonby
Newton Morrell
Barton
Croft-on-Tees
Dalton-on-Tees
Eryholme
Girsby
Picton
Crath
Ravensworth
Scotch Corner Services
Sockburn

At-a-glance...

Walk	Page	Start	Nat. Grid Reference	Distance	Height Gain	Time
Alston and the South Tyne Valley	64	Alston Station	NY 716467	6¼ miles (10km)	475ft (145m)	3 hrs
Appleby, Rutter Force and the River Eden	70	Appleby-in-Westmorland	NY 683204	8½ miles (13.7km)	490ft (150m)	4½ hrs
Armathwaite, Coombs Wood and Ainstable	28	Armathwaite	NY 506461	5½ miles (8.9km)	640ft (195m)	3 hrs
Around Dufton Pike	38	Dufton	NY 689249	5 miles (8km)	625ft (190m)	2½ hrs
Auckland Park, Escomb and the River Wear	49	Bishop Auckland	NZ 211301	7½ miles (12.1km)	625ft (190m)	3½ hrs
Barnard Castle, Cotherstone and the River Tees	73	Barnard Castle	NZ 050163	8½ miles (13.7km)	575ft (175m)	4½ hrs
Bowes Moor	86	Bowes	NY 995134	10½ miles (16.9km)	785ft (240m)	5½ hrs
Castle Eden Dene	20	Castle Eden Dene Visitor Centre	NZ 427393	2½ miles (4km)	360ft (110m)	1½ hrs
Cauldron Snout	55	Cow Green Reservoir	NY 810309	7¼ miles (11.7km)	560ft (170m)	3½ hrs
Causey Arch and Beamish Woods	33	Beamish Country Park	NZ 204561	5 miles (8km)	655ft (200m)	2½ hrs
Cox Green and Penshaw Hill	18	Cox Green	NZ 326552	3½ miles (5.6km)	445ft (135m)	1½ hrs
Crossthwaite Common, Rake Gill and Holwick	82	Middleton-in-Teesdale	NY 947254	9½ miles (15.3km)	1,375ft (420m)	5 hrs
Durham – Riverside and Woods	30	Durham, Market Place	NZ 273425	4½ miles (7.2km)	215ft (65m)	2½ hrs
Egglestone Abbey, Paradise and the Meeting of the Waters	52	Egglestone Abbey, nr Barnard Castle	NZ 062150	7 miles (11.3km)	215ft (65m)	3 hrs
Hamsterley Forest	36	Hamsterley Forest Visitor Centre	NZ 091312	5 miles (8km)	670ft (205m)	2½ hrs
High and Low Force	77	Middleton-in-Teesdale	NY 907282	8½ miles (13.7km)	900ft (275m)	4½ hrst
High Cup Nick	80	Dufton	NY 689249	8 miles (12.9km)	1,445ft (440m)	4 hrs
Kirkby Stephen and Nateby	40	Kirkby Stephen	NY 775087	6½ miles (10.5km)	475ft (145m)	3½ hrs
Marsden Rock and Whitburn	46	Marsden Bay	NZ 397650	7 miles (11.3km)	375ft (115m)	3½ hrs
Smardale Gill	22	Smardale	NY 739082	4½ miles (7.2km)	360ft (110m)	2½ hrs
St John's Chapel and Westgate	26	St John's Chapel	NY 886378	4½ miles (7.2km)	425ft (130m)	2 hrs
Staindrop	24	Staindrop	NZ 128205	4½ miles (7.2km)	260ft (80m)	2½ hrs
Stanhope	14	Stanhope	NY 995392	2½ miles (4km)	115ft (35m)	1¼ hrs
Sunbiggin Tarn and Great Asby Scar	43	Sunbiggin Tarn	NY 675078	6¾ miles (10.9km)	510ft (155m)	3½ hrs
Talkin Tarn and Gelt Woods	58	Talkin Tarn Country Park	NY 543591	6 miles (9.7km)	310ft (95m)	3 hrs
Waskerley Way	67	Waskerley	NZ 050453	7½ miles (12.1km)	705ft (215m)	4 hrs
Wolsingham and the Weardale Way	61	Wolsingham	NZ 073366	7½ miles (12.1km)	785ft (240m)	3 hrs
Wynyard Woodland Park and Thorpe Wood	16	Wynyard Woodland Park	NZ 402243	3½ miles (5.6km)	215ft (65m)	1½ hrs

Comments

On the outward leg, the Pennine Way is followed through the austere terrain of the South Tyne valley; the return is alongside the track of the South Tynedale Railway.

This beautiful and varied walk in the Eden valley visits an impressive waterfall, passes through a remote village with an interesting church, and finishes with a lovely stroll beside the river.

Rising through the sylvan gorge of the River Eden, this walk reveals fine panoramas along the highest ridge of the Pennine chain and across to the Lake District's northern mountains.

After an initial walk through a gorge, the route encircles the base of the conically shaped Dufton Pike. There are magnificent views of the North Pennines and across the Eden valley to the Lakeland fells.

There is plenty of historic interest on this walk in the Wear valley. It includes the palace and former hunting ground of the Bishops of Durham, a Victorian viaduct and a Saxon church.

An outstandingly attractive Teesdale walk, which keeps above the river for most of the way, apart from the final stretch where you descend to the wooded banks of the Tees.

There is a tremendous feeling of spaciousness and isolation on this route which, apart from an opening stretch beside the River Greta, is entirely across open and exposed moorland.

The walk takes you along both sides of one of the steep-sided and thickly wooded denes that run down to the Durham coast.

There are easier ways of reaching Cauldron Snout but this route provides real excitement as the path follows the River Tees through an ever-narrowing gorge to the foot of the waterfall.

The world's earliest railway bridge, which spans a wooded gorge, is the main focal point of this route. There is fine woodland walking, and the route passes by Beamish Open Air Museum.

The Doric temple on Penshaw Hill is the climax of this Weardale walk. It was built as a memorial to 'Radical' Jack Lambton, the Liberal politician who died in 1840, and is a magnificent viewpoint.

The middle part of this triangular walk follows a little-used bridleway over grouse moors so a compass may prove useful. Both of the other legs are straightforward, the return being on the banks of the Tees.

Much attractive riverside and woodland walking is enhanced by the dramatic views of Durham Cathedral and Castle, rising above the River Wear at both the start and finish.

This walk follows both banks of the River Tees past a famous beauty spot, the Meeting of the Waters, where the River Greta joins the Tees. It provided the subject for one of Turner's finest landscapes.

An undulating ramble through County Durham's largest forest, with fine woodland and beckside walking and grand views to enfolding moors and ridges.

High Force has a drop of 70ft (21m) and is the mightiest of English waterfalls. This walk takes you to its best viewpoint and then follows the Tees upstream. The return is on lanes and field paths.

From Dufton a steady climb along the Pennine Way leads to a dramatic chasm. On the return you enjoy the most superb views across the Eden valley to the Lakeland fells.

There is a series of impressive views of both the North Pennines and the Howgills on this Eden valley walk. The opening stretch is by the river.

The walk first heads inland over the gentle slopes of the Cleadon Hills and finishes with an exhilarating walk along the coast, passing by a series of rocky and sandy bays.

Enjoy spectacular views of the Howgill Fells, followed by an elevated walk along a disused railway through the National Nature Reserve of Smardale Gill.

This walk in Upper Weardale passes by remains of former lead mines and finishes with a pleasant stroll by the river.

Starting from one of Durham's prettiest villages, the walk takes you across fields, by streams and alongside woodland.

Fine views up and down the River Wear can be enjoyed on this short walk around Stanhope.

From a lonely, sun-dappled tarn the walk rises to cross the unworldly landscape of a huge limestone pavement, returning via a Neolithic stone circle.

The tranquil beauty of Talkin Tarn is enjoyed at the start and finish; in between there is a dramatic walk through a thickly wooded gorge.

Unlike many of the longer walks in this book, this one can be attempted when conditions are less than perfect. It uses a long section of disused railway as well as field and woodland paths.

This is a long walk with no severe gradients. It provides an opportunity to enjoy the scenery of Weardale, which can be just as attractive as that of Teesdale to the south.

Starting at a former railway station, the combination of a disused railway track and pleasant woodland makes for an attractive and interesting walk.

Introduction to Durham, North Pennines and Tyne & Wear

For centuries the main route across the North Pennines has been through the Stainmore Gap, now occupied by the busy A66, and at its highest point is the county boundary between Cumbria and Durham. At both ends of the gap – Brough in the west and Bowes in the east – are the remains of Norman castles situated within the earthworks of earlier Roman forts, a clear indication of the strategic importance of this route.

This *Pathfinder Guide* covers both the Cumbrian and Durham sides of the North Pennines, a designated Area of Outstanding Natural Beauty, and also extends eastwards across Durham to the North Sea coast. It embraces the traditional – pre-1974 – boundaries of County Durham, i.e. all the land between the Tees and the Tyne, and therefore includes the areas of the metropolitan county of Tyne & Wear to the south of the Tyne, as well as parts of former Cleveland to the north of the Tees.

Castles and churches

For much of its history this has been a frontier zone. Just to the north is Hadrian's Wall and there are several remains of Roman forts in the area. Medieval castles are in abundance: some of the finest are at Brough, Brougham and Appleby in Cumbria, and Barnard Castle, Bowes and Raby in County Durham, plus, of course, the great episcopal castle at Durham itself. After the union of the crowns in 1603 largely ended centuries of war with Scotland, these castles either became picturesque ruins or were converted into more comfortable residences. Durham Castle was given a different role; in 1836 the bishop gave it to the new University of Durham as its foundation college.

In the Anglo-Saxon period, the region was the heartland of early Northumbrian Christianity and today contains some of the finest surviving Saxon churches in England. Two in particular are the tiny church at Escomb in the Wear valley and the church and monastic site at Jarrow, where the Venerable Bede, 'Father of English History', lived and worked. This is now part of the fascinating and imaginative Jarrow Hall complex.

A focal point of the region is the city of Durham, one of Britain's finest and most attractive historic cities. The cathedral – described by Sir Walter Scott as 'half church of God, half castle 'gainst the Scot' – and castle stand side by side on a wooded cliff above a horseshoe bend in the River Wear. They make an unforgettable sight and have deservedly been given World Heritage status. It was in 995, after many years of wandering from place to place, that the remains of St Cuthbert found a permanent home here and the diocese was established. In the late 11th century the Normans erected the mighty cathedral, one of the finest in Europe, and built the castle, twin symbols of the enormous power exercised by the

The Tees below Bracken Rigg

Introduction

medieval bishops of Durham. They were prince bishops – a phrase much used by the local tourist authorities to promote the area – granted virtually sovereign powers by Norman kings in return for protecting this vulnerable border area from Scottish invasions. The bishops raised their own armies and taxes, minted their own coinage and had their own courts.

Industry and towns

Industry has always been a major factor in this area. From the 16th century onwards, lead-mining flourished in the remote valleys and hills of the North Pennines, reaching its height in the Victorian era. This has now gone, but the remains of some of the mines can still be seen, especially in Upper Weardale, and there are lead-mining museums at Killhope and Nenthead.

The biggest impact of all on the landscape of the region was the development of the Durham coalfield and the growth of shipbuilding on the Tyne and Wear, both reaching their zenith during the Industrial Revolution. This was one of Britain's most prolific coal-producing areas, and the mines even extended to the coast and under the sea. Transporting the coal to the nearest rivers – Tyne, Wear and Tees – was a major problem and this was overcome by the creation of wooden waggonways, the forerunners of the railways, pioneered in this part of the country. Causey Arch, near Stanley, claims to be the world's earliest-surviving railway bridge, and George Stephenson's Stockton to Darlington Railway, opened in 1825, was the first railway in the world to use steam-powered locomotives.

During the Industrial Revolution the medieval city of Durham was soon outgrown by the rise of the industrial towns of Gateshead, Stockton and Darlington and the great ports of South Shields, Sunderland and Hartlepool, the latter group mostly engaged in coal exporting and ship-building. Now the coal mines and shipyards have gone and the Industrial Revolution has largely receded into history, but an excellent way of appreciating the industrial heritage of the area is to spend a day at the Open Air Museum at Beamish, not far from the Causey Arch, a living and working experience of life in the North of England at the beginning of the 20th century.

Geography

Tourist literature describes the North Pennines as 'England's last wilderness' and there is some justification in that claim. It is an excellent walking area and one that tends to get neglected in favour of the nearby Lake District, Yorkshire Dales and Northumberland National Parks. Its huge expanses of wild and open moorland include some of the highest peaks in the Pennine range, and on both sides sparkling rivers wind their way through lovely dales and across lush lowland pastures to the sea. There are also remote and unspoilt villages and fine market towns: Barnard Castle, Kirkby Stephen, Appleby and Alston. The latter is the highest in England and is often cut off during a hard winter.

On the western slopes is the lovely valley of the Eden, and the river eventually flows through Carlisle and on into the Solway Firth. From the higher points, magnificent views extend over the Eden valley to the outline of the Lakeland mountains and on across the Solway to the Galloway hills on the horizon. To the south, the shapely, grassy summits of the secluded Howgill Fells link the Pennines to the Lake District; the area was added to the Yorkshire Dales National Park in August 2016.

For first time visitors to the area, perhaps expecting nothing but coal mines and industrial towns, County Durham may well come as something of a pleasant surprise. Extending eastwards from the slopes of the Pennines are Teesdale and Weardale, as beautiful as any of the better-known dales of Yorkshire and Derbyshire and well-wooded in their lower reaches. Between Teesdale and Weardale are the wooded expanses of Hamsterley Forest, a fine recreational area with superb walking facilities. The Wear valley and the area to the north was the heart of the Durham coalfield but the mines have closed and most of the area has been landscaped and made green again.

East Durham is noted for its denes, thickly wooded and steep-sided valleys, which stretch like fingers to the North Sea coast. The coast itself, despite being heavily urbanised and industrialised, is not without its attractions. There are fine sandy beaches and a particularly dramatic stretch in Tyne & Wear between South Shields and Sunderland, with a series of stacks and rock arches, including the famous Marsden Rock.

Walking in the area

The Pennine Way weaves its way across the North Pennines, both making use of the river valleys and taking a high-level moorland route in places. There are other waymarked long-distance paths – Teesdale Way and

Weardale Way – and in County Durham there is a network of former railway tracks that have been converted into footpaths and cycleways, many of them originally built to link the coal mines with the main rail network.

Visitors to the area will find walks to suit all tastes and all levels of fitness. The North Pennines may well be 'England's last wilderness' but both here and in County Durham there is much more than wild moorland. Walkers can

Dufton Pike, from the walk to High Cup Nick

enjoy the challenge of some of the finest moorland terrain in the country if they wish, but for the less ambitious, or if the weather is unsuitable – always a crucial factor to take into consideration – there are plenty of more relaxing, low-level walks beside the rivers Tees, Wear and Eden, through woodlands and forests, by the coast and along some of the former railway tracks.

This book includes a list of waypoints alongside the description of the walk, so that you can enjoy the full benefits of gps should you wish to. For more information on using your gps, read the *Pathfinder® Guide GPS for Walkers*, by gps teacher and navigation trainer, Clive Thomas (ISBN 978-0-7117-4445-5). For essential information on map reading and basic navigation, read the *Pathfinder® Guide Map Reading Skills* by outdoor writer, Terry Marsh (ISBN 978-0-7117-4978-8). Both titles are available in bookshops or can be ordered online at www.pathfinderwalks.co.uk

Stanhope

		GPS waypoints	
Start	Stanhope	📝	NY 995 392
Distance	2½ miles (4km)	Ⓐ	NY 996 390
Height gain	115ft (35m)	Ⓑ	NZ 001 383
Approximate time	1¼ hours	Ⓒ	NY 995 388
Parking	Durham Dales Centre, Stanhope	Ⓓ	NY 991 391
Ordnance Survey maps	Landranger 92 (Barnard Castle), Explorer OL31 (North Pennines – Teesdale & Weardale)		

This short and easy walk in Weardale is mainly along riverside paths and across meadows on both banks of the Wear. There are attractive views up and downstream and across the river to Stanhope from the south bank. The walk necessitates crossing stepping stones at one point but if the river is high or the stones are likely to be slippery, there is an easier alternative crossing via a footbridge.

The former quarrying and lead-mining village of Stanhope stands on the north bank of the River Wear. In the church-yard of the fine 12th-century church is the stump of a fossilised tree, placed here in 1962 and thought to be around 250 million years old. On the opposite side of the Market Place is Stanhope Castle, a large house built in the late 18th century. The walk starts at the Durham Dales Centre, which comprises a tourist information centre, shop, craft workshops and tearoom.

📝 Begin by walking down to the road and turn left into the Market Place. Bear right along the Butts, by the **Packhorse Inn**, follow the road around a right bend and, before reaching the river, turn left Ⓐ – still along the Butts – to join the bank of the Wear.

Go through a metal kissing-gate to cross a railway line, go through another gate, bear left across a field and go through a kissing-gate on the far side. Keep along the right edge of the next field, go through a kissing-gate in the corner, continue in the same direction across the corner of a sports field to rejoin the riverbank and bear left along it. Go through a kissing-gate in the field corner, recross the railway line, turn right through another kissing-gate and walk along a fence-lined path to yet another kissing-gate. After going through that, continue along the right edge of a field and climb a stile onto a lane Ⓑ.

Turn right to cross first a bridge over the river and then a railway bridge and, where the lane turns left, turn right, at public footpath and Weardale Way signs, along a tarmac track through a caravan site. At the far end of the site – 'Hazel Corner' – keep ahead to climb a gate-side stile into an area of woodland. The roughening track drops gradually through the trees high above the Wear; on emerging from the woods bend right to use a stile and walk beside a wall on your left to a sharp corner. Ⓒ Turn left beside the fence and walk the field edge

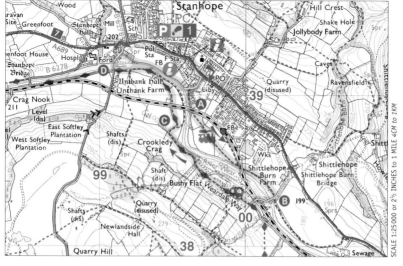

| 0 | 200 | 400 | 600 | 800 METRES | 1 |
| 0 | 200 | 400 | 600 YARDS | ½ |

KILOMETRES
MILES

to cross the Weardale Railway via two concrete ladder-stiles. The well-worn path beyond leads beneath trees to a gate into a tarred lane; bear left along this.

If you do not wish to use stepping stones (or if the Wear is running high), cross the footbridge you'll shortly reach on your right and turn right off the far end to rejoin the full route.

Otherwise, stay on the tarred lane to a junction **D**; here turn right to use the long string of stepping stones beside a ford through the river. Walk ahead from the far end for 150 yds to take a tarred track on your right. This runs between a playground and the wall of an outdoor swimming pool before becoming a riverside promenade. Remain with this to the road and bear left, uphill, to return to the Market Place and the nearby Durham Dales Centre. ●

The River Wear at Stanhope

Wynyard Woodland Park and Thorpe Wood

Start	Wynyard Woodland Park & Planetarium, signposted from A177 between Sedgefield and Stockton-on-Tees
Distance	3½ miles (5.6km)
Height gain	215ft (65m)
Approximate time	1½ hours
Parking	Country Park Visitor Centre
Ordnance Survey maps	Landranger 93 (Middlesbrough), Explorers 305 (Bishop Auckland) and 306 (Middlesbrough & Hartlepool)

GPS waypoints

- NZ 402 243
- Ⓐ NZ 400 254
- Ⓑ NZ 397 253
- Ⓒ NZ 407 254
- Ⓓ NZ 409 243
- Ⓔ NZ 404 247

The walk begins with a pleasant and easy stroll along the track of a disused railway. It continues across fields and ends with a ramble through the beautiful Thorpe Wood, a nature reserve. In such tranquil surroundings, it is difficult to believe that industrial Teesside is so close, but on the more open middle section of the route the views extend right across Teesside to the line of the Cleveland Hills.

Thorpe Pond

Based at the old Thorpe Thewles station, the Country Park (also known as the Castle Eden Walkway) is a network of secluded paths and cycle tracks at the edge of Teesside. The former railway, opened in the 1870s and closed in 1966, was mainly a mineral railway that carried coal from the Durham coalfield to staithes on the Tees Estuary. Thorpe Wood is a significant survival of the north east's semi-natural ancient woodland. Adjacent to the old station are an observatory and planetarium (for programme details see www.wynyard-planetarium.net).

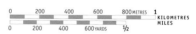 Stand on the old platform with your back to the tearoom door and turn right. Drop down onto the old railway and walk north, through the gate and along the track bed. Count the over-bridges; at the third one climb the steps immediately past it on the left and rise to a rough lane Ⓐ. If the trees are not in leaf, a short detour to the right along the lane reveals the ruins of 12th century Grindon Church Ⓑ, in trees off to your right (no public access).

Back at the old over-bridge, cross it and, at the nearby fork, keep ahead through an open gateway, well-waymarked as the route of Cycle Route 1 for the Tees Barrage & Thorpe Thewles. This is a wide track along the left edge of a field. Trace this through a neck of woodland and onward as a headland track between open fields. At a straggle of (mostly dead) trees Ⓒ, bend right along the track, remaining with it to crest a low rise. Views ahead extend beyond the industrial complexes of Teesside to the shapely forms of the Cleveland Hills and North Yorkshire Moors beyond the hidden Tees Estuary. At a T-junction near an isolated farm, turn right and drop down into the shallow valley.

Upon reaching a fenced compound on your left, turn right Ⓓ through a gate to join a wide path through Thorpe Wood Nature Reserve. Just past the reedy Thorpe Pond, turn left Ⓔ at the waymarked junction. The path crosses a burn and bends right to climb a lengthy series of steps. Bend left up more steps to reach a gate at the near-end of a bridge. Use the hand-gate and drop left, down to the old railway trackbed. Turn left to return to the Visitor Centre. ●

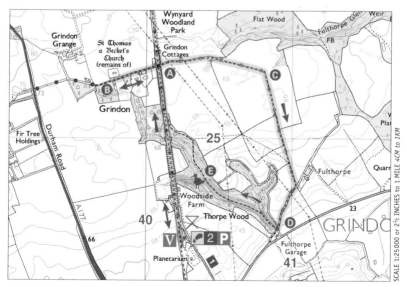

Cox Green and Penshaw Hill

		GPS waypoints
Start	Cox Green, 3 miles (4.8km) west of Sunderland	🖉 NZ 326 552
Distance	3½ miles (5.6km)	Ⓐ NZ 320 546
Height gain	445ft (135m)	Ⓑ NZ 321 538
Approximate time	1½ hours	Ⓒ NZ 324 544
Parking	Cox Green	Ⓓ NZ 329 539
Ordnance Survey maps	Landranger 88 (Newcastle upon Tyne), Explorer 308 (Durham & Sunderland)	Ⓔ NZ 334 543
		Ⓕ NZ 337 548
		Ⓖ NZ 334 554

The imposing temple monument on Penshaw Hill draws the eye from afar, whilst the hill itself is a superb viewpoint. The hill is also claimed as the place where the celebrated Lambton Worm lurked – the (hardly visible) terraces ringing the summit are said to be the result of the worm-like dragon coiling itself around it. The walk links this folk-tale location with an old port beside the River Wear.

Cox Green's peaceful situation belies its genesis as a thriving boat-building centre and port shipping coal, timber and sandstone in Victorian times. The remains of substantial quays line the Wear's banks, and mooring pontoons are still used by leisure craft. An information board near the Oddfellows Arms identifies the major local sites.

🖉 Turn left along the riverside lane, pass by a footbridge to your right and walk in front of the strand of houses that make up Cox Green. Beyond the houses, remain on the riverside path, the Weardale Way. In the woods on your left, low stone arches mark the end of tunnels from Low Lambton quarries, along which sandstone was carried on tram roads to the quays here. At an information board 100 yds before reaching the Victoria Viaduct, turn left

Ⓐ on a path that meanders up a wooded valley. Go through a gate and keep right, use the tunnel beneath the railway embankment and follow this rough lane through to a road Ⓑ.

Turn left along Coxgreen Road; in about 700 yds turn right at a fingerpost Ⓒ, climb a stile and walk up the field-side path beside a hedge/fence on your right. About halfway up, swap sides and continue uphill to use a stile into a lane. Turn left; in 100 yds turn left along the footpath signed for Penshaw Hill Ⓓ – there are two village pubs a farther 150 yds along the road here. This path rises very gradually across the flank of Penshaw Hill; views stretch over the massive Nissan car plant to the coast and north to the distant Cheviot Hills. At a major junction of paths at a woodland-edge gate, take the path

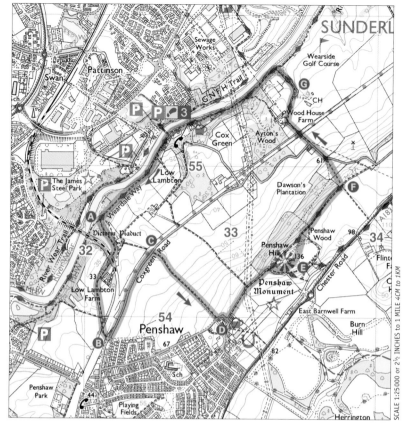

SCALE 1:25000 or 2½ INCHES to 1 MILE 4CM to 1KM

```
0    200   400   600   800 METRES   1
                                     KILOMETRES
                                     MILES
0    200   400   600 YARDS   ½
```

half-left, up steps and through a hand-gate. Trace the wood-side fence for 50 paces and then fork right, climbing further steps to reach the Penshaw Monument **E**.

This Doric-style temple, based on the ancient Temple of Hephaestus in Athens, was built in 1844 as a memorial to John 'Radical Jack' Lambton, First Earl of Durham and a Liberal parliamentary champion of the *Great Reform Act* of 1832. The story of the Lambton Worm is one of the most famous north-country folk tales. John, the heir to the Lambton estates in medieval times, is said to have slain the monstrous worm-dragon but, in doing so, invoked a witch's curse under which the next nine lords of

Lambton would die unexpected deaths. And none of the next nine Lords of Lambton died in their beds.

Passing to the left of the monument as you approached it, a wide grassy path drops down to a kissing-gate, beyond which follow the path beside the woods on your left. At the end of the woods climb a stile **F**; turn downhill, cross another stile and head towards the golf clubhouse. Join a lane at a corner and turn left. Keep ahead at a junction along the 'No Through Road' and bend right with this alongside a fairway. As it bends right again to approach the clubhouse, fork left **G** along the waymarked footpath into the trees. The path descends alongside a secluded, wooded beck to meet the Weardale Way; turn left along the riverbank to return to Cox Green. ●

Castle Eden Dene

Castle Eden Dene

		GPS waypoints
Start	Castle Eden Dene Visitor Centre on Stanhope Chase, just south of Peterlee and signed from the town and the A19	✎ NZ 427 393 Ⓐ NZ 427 390 Ⓑ NZ 418 387
Distance	2½ miles (4km)	
Height gain	360ft (110m)	
Approximate time	1½ hours	
Parking	Oakerside Dene Lodge	
Ordnance Survey maps	Landranger 93 (Middlesbrough), Explorer 308 (Durham & Sunderland)	

The Dene is a precious survivor of the wild wood that once covered much of England and is the largest area of semi-natural woodland in the North East. The woodlands and ravine are home to over 450 species of plants (some spectacular ferns here) and are one of the few places in England where red squirrels still retain a foothold. The walk follows steep, sometimes narrow paths, steps and footbridges that may be slippery in wet weather. *One footbridge arches 80ft (24m) above the gorge.*

Castle Eden Dene, now a National Nature Reserve, is one of a number of well-wooded ravines that stretch through the countryside of east Durham down to the North Sea coast. Its natural appearance is something of a deception because in the 18th century the dene

was landscaped by the Burdon family, local landowners, in the 'Picturesque' style that was fashionable at the time, attempting to re-create on the Durham

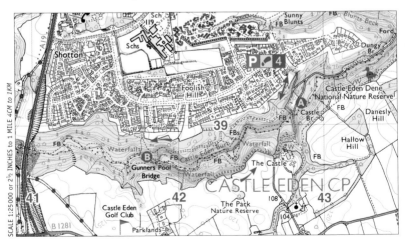

Castle Eden Dene

coast the idealised landscape of Italy. Many of the present paths and bridges over the burn were constructed at this time.

From the car park, go down the ramp at the corner opposite the Visitor Centre and go through the kissing-gate beside the National Nature Reserve noticeboard. Take the track ahead, which curves right and descends into the wooded dene and, at a fork, continue along the left-hand track down to Castle Bridge Ⓐ. Do not cross it but turn right onto an undulating path above Castle Eden Burn, curving left to cross a footbridge over it below almost vertical cliffs.

Continue – now with the burn on the right – and the path climbs, via steps in places, passing more sheer cliffs. Ignoring a path coming in from the left, descend to the burn again, turn right to recross it and follow the path to the left, climbing steeply and bearing slightly

left on meeting another path. At a fork, take the left-hand, lower path which descends and, when you see a footbridge (Gunner's Pool Bridge), turn left and head down steps to cross it Ⓑ. This is a beautiful spot, with the burn far below cascading over rocks at the bottom of the gorge.

Turn left off the bridge, joining the Red Squirrel waymarked route. The path rises gently through the woods, at one point crossing a culvert. Keep right at a minor junction, briefly reaching the top edge of the woods beside a metal-rail fence before falling gradually again to arrive at a gate into a tarred lane. Do not go through this, but turn left along the woodland path. Keep left at a junction, remaining on this path through oak, lime and yew woods above a deep little valley on your left to reach and cross Castle Bridge. Bear left; ignore the path left at Ⓐ and climb up the wide main path back to the start. ●

24 miles
35 mins → M6

Smardale Gill

Start	Smardale, 2½ miles (4km) west of Kirkby Stephen, signed from A685	**GPS waypoints**
Distance	4½ miles (7.2km)	✎ NY 739 082
Height gain	360ft (110m)	Ⓐ NY 735 066
Approximate time	2½ hours	Ⓑ NY 720 059
Parking	Smardale National Nature Reserve car park, off Beck Lane and signed for Crosby Garrett (honesty box nearby)	Ⓒ NY 722 062
Ordnance Survey maps	Landranger 91 (Appleby-in-Westmorland), Explorer OL19 (Howgill Fells & Upper Eden Valley)	

A gentle climb onto Smardale Fell reveals extraordinary views of The Howgill Fells and the mountains of the north-eastern Lake District. The walk then drops into remote Smardale Gill, joining a disused railway on embankments and across a viaduct through the glorious, wooded gorge of Scandal Beck, a National Nature Reserve renowned for wildflowers, butterflies and a colony of red squirrels.

✎ Turn right from the car park entrance, right again across the old railway bridge and right once more

Smardale packhorse bridge

along the 'No Through Road', passing the imposing Smardale Hall with its turrets and thick walls. Pass beneath the railway and follow the tarred lane to its end beside a cottage. Go through the waymarked field gate here – a bridleway to Brownber – and fork right, rising beside a wall to reach a copse. Peel away left along the grassy old track, rising gently to use a field gate. Remain on the track, keeping a wall on your right. Go through a gate just up from a corner and continue beside the wall on your right. Looking back you will see tremendous views across the Eden Valley to the line of the Pennines. Bend right with the wall, shortly reaching a fingerpost at a junction of bridleways Ⓐ.

Turn right towards Smardale Bridge. The way rises very gently to its highest point near a stand of trees (which are beyond two walls). Ahead now is a

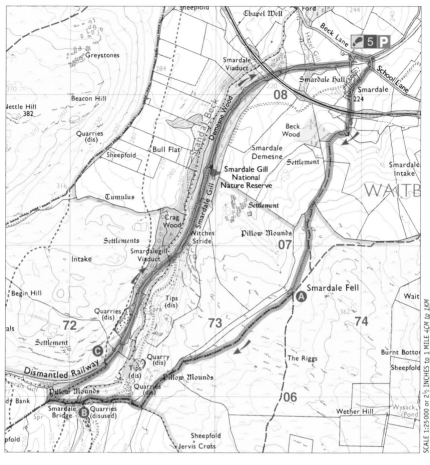

SCALE 1:25000 or 2½ INCHES to 1 MILE 4CM to 1KM

majestic view of the Howgill Fells, whilst the far horizon ahead right is formed by the Shap Fells and the mountains above Haweswater. Heading downhill, climb a ladder-stile beside a sheepfold and trace the track beside a wall; it soon swings right to a gate. Use this and drop down to the solid old Smardale packhorse bridge over Scandal Beck **B**. The beck is known to be home to otters and the endangered white-clawed crayfish; look out for dippers (blackbird-sized birds with a white bib) and wagtails here.

Cross the bridge and turn right at the fingerpost onto the steep path signed C-to-C (Coast to Coast), rising diagonally up the slope to put a wall, then fence on your left. Follow this to an over-bridge across the disused railway; at the near bridge corner climb the stile **C** on your left, descend steps and turn right beneath the bridge. The line linked the coalfields of the north east with the iron and steel works at Barrow-in-Furness; it's now a superb, elevated walkway through the limestone gorge and woodlands of Smardale Gill.

Interpretation boards along the way explain and highlight the myriad features to be seen and creatures and flowers to be looked for. Simply remain on the track bed, shortly crossing the curving Smardalegill Viaduct, to return to the car park 1¼ miles (2km) away. ●

Staindrop

Start	Staindrop Post office	**GPS waypoints**	
Distance	4½ miles (7.2km)	✐	NZ 128 205
Height gain	260ft (80m)	Ⓐ	NZ 127 204
		Ⓑ	NZ 124 198
Approximate time	2½ hours	Ⓒ	NZ 108 196
Parking	Roadside in Staindrop	Ⓓ	NZ 108 201
Ordnance Survey maps	Landranger 92 (Barnard Castle), Explorer 304 (Darlington & Richmond)	Ⓔ	NZ 102 200
		Ⓕ	NZ 102 208

Much of the first part of this well-waymarked and mainly flat walk is by the banks of the delightful Sudburn Beck. The route then continues across fields and along the edge of woodland to return to Staindrop, a most attractive village. From many points there are fine views across the surrounding countryside.

Staindrop is an outstanding example of a 'green village' – a characteristic of County Durham – with long, wide greens enclosed by mostly 17th- and 18th-century buildings. At the east end of the village is the impressive medieval church, the 'Cathedral of the Dales', which dates back to the Norman period but was extended and rebuilt in succeeding centuries. Inside are the tombs of some of the powerful Neville family, who lived at nearby Raby Castle, a clue as to why such a large and imposing church should be found in this relatively small village.

✐ With your back to the post office, turn left and then fork half-left alongside South Green. Turn left along the narrow lane – Stangarth Lane – beside the Scarth Memorial Hall and walk to a path junction Ⓐ at the end, near Nursery Garage. Turn right, walk to a gate-side stile, climb it and bear half-left, aiming left of the new housing which direction finds a stile and slab bridge to cross. Continue in-line, crossing a culvert and a hand-gate and

keep ahead to the left of the in-field oak to a stone step-stile onto a road Ⓑ.

Cross the road, climb a stone stile, walk across a field to climb another one and continue along a path beside the tree-lined bank of Sudburn Beck. Keep by the beck, along the edge of meadows and over a succession of stiles, finally climbing steps onto a road to the right

of Sudburn Bridge. Cross over, pass beside a gate, climb the stone stile in front and bear slightly left across a field to a stile. Climb it and continue in the same direction across the next field to rejoin the beck. After climbing a stile, look out in the next field for where you turn left over another stile to continue beside the beck. Climb a stile, keep ahead to go through a gate and just beyond that is a footbridge over the beck 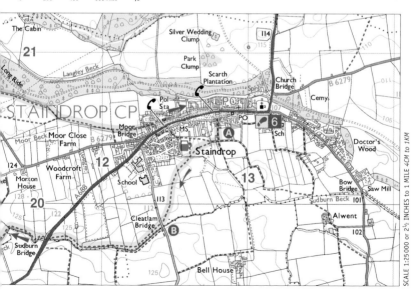.

Do not cross the bridge; instead turn right and follow the track uphill, then walk to the top-right corner of the field and use the hand-gate. Turn left to the adjoining stile, once over which turn right to trace the inside edge of the paddock all the way round to a stile into the driveway. Turn right along this, from which there are good views across to Staindrop and ahead to the Raby Castle Estate. Just before the drive bends right, go through the waymarked gate on the left **D** and walk the left edge of the field to go through a gate into the next pasture. From here aim half-right, climbing over the low rise and heading for the far right corner and an oak tree **E**.

Do not use the gate beneath the oak; instead look right for another (way-marked) gate 20 paces in-field from the corner. Go through this and head directly across two fields to reach Scaife House Farm. Enter the farmyard, walk left of the farmhouse and wind with the driveway to reach the main road **F**.

Turn right, and at a public footpath sign in 200 yds turn left along the drive to West Lodge. Just before reaching the Lodge, use a gate on your right to join the path beside Ladyclose Wood (on your left) through several fields. Beyond a second lodge house, remain wood-side for another three fields. As the woods bend left and the third pasture narrows, peel right to a stone stile in the far corner. Climb it, walk along the right edge of two fields and about half-way across the second one, use the stile on your right to access a narrow, enclosed path. Follow this to the left; it presently encounters a squeezer-stile, beyond which keep ahead to emerge at the west end of Staindrop's North Green. Walk on towards the distant church to return to the start. ●

```
0      200    400    600   800 METRES   1
                                        KILOMETRES
                                        MILES
0      200    400    600 YARDS    ½
```

St John's Chapel and Westgate

		GPS waypoints
Start	St John's Chapel, Weardale	 NY 886 378
Distance	4½ miles (7.2km)	Ⓐ NY 885 381
Height gain	425ft (130m)	Ⓑ NY 888 386
Approximate time	2 hours	Ⓒ NY 901 390
Parking	Just east of St John's Chapel livestock market	Ⓓ NY 905 380
		Ⓔ NY 895 380
Ordnance Survey maps	Landrangers 91 (Appleby-in-Westmorland) or 92 (Barnard Castle), Explorer OL31 (North Pennines – Teesdale & Weardale)	

From the village of St John's Chapel, the route heads uphill and continues along the north side of Weardale, passing by abandoned quarries and former lead mines before descending into Westgate. Most of the remainder of the walk is along or close to the banks of the River Wear. There are fine views over Upper Weardale and some pleasant riverside walking.

Now a quiet backwater, St John's Chapel was once a busy town and important centre of lead-mining and quarrying in Upper Weardale. The Georgian church, on the site of the original medieval chapel, and Victorian town hall are evidence of its former heyday.

From the car park, turn left along

The River Tees at Daddry Shield

the road into the Market Place, where you turn right along a lane that passes between the church on the right and town hall on the left. In 200 yds the road bends right at Burn Foot; here turn left Ⓐ beside a horse trough, cross the narrow bridge over a burn and turn immediately right to reach a kissing-gate at the end of a short drive.

Go through, take the tarmac path across a field and cross a footbridge over the River Wear. Keep ahead to continue alongside a wall, climb steps, go through a kissing-gate, continue up more steps and, at the top, keep straight ahead across a field and climb a stone stile onto a lane. Cross over and use the hand-gate beside the gated track to High Fairhills. Walk up the track until it bends right; on the left here use the narrow stile through a wall and head half-right up a grassy path to a gap in a wall. Pass through and head left up the

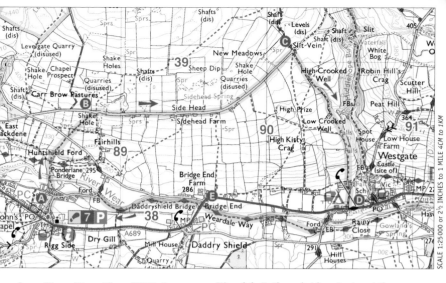

SCALE 1:25 000 or 2½ INCHES to 1 MILE 4CM to 1KM

0	200	400	600	800 METRES	1	
						KILOMETRES
						MILES
0	200	400	600 YARDS	½		

steep pasture to a small hand-gate and steps onto a lane **B**.

Turn right and keep along the lane to where it ends, a distance of about 1 mile (1.6km). All the way there are fine views to the right across Upper Weardale, and you pass the remains of some of the abandoned quarries and former lead mines for which this area was famous in the 19th century. On reaching the end of the lane, turn right **C** through a gate beside a barn, joining a rough track which drops through gates and passes a barn under renovation to end beside gates to a substantial house. Ahead left here is a hand-gate; use this and walk down the marshy pasture to a similar hand-gate and immediately following field-gate. Continue downhill, passing right of the ruin through a stand of trees. The sunken track falls to a gate into a farmyard; go through this and walk the walled lane to the main road in Westgate **D**.

The village microbrewery pub is to the left; this walk turns right. In 100yds turn left (at postbox) on the lane signed 'Ford'; cross the footbridge and rise between the abutments of the former Weardale Railway bridge. Just past the cottage turn right on the waymarked Weardale Way. Pass in front of the next cottages to use a kissing-gate into a meadow. Head to the right of the distant buildings to take another kissing-gate, keep a fence on your left and use a hand-gate into a rough lane in front of cottages.

As this turns left, look right for an ornate hand-gate at the edge of a garden area, walk to the footbridge at the far side of the patch, cross this, a stile and a flat bridge and then walk ahead on a path above the Wear. This is the old railway track bed; remain on this until the far end of the strip of trees on your left. Here, gradually angle right off the embankment, aiming for a hand-gate and flight of steps up onto the river bridge at Daddry Shield **E**.

Cross the road but not the bridge, climb the barrier and drop down the steps (Weardale Way) and cross a footbridge to join an initially fenced riverside path. This becomes a peaceful transit linking a series of rapids, shoots and falls to reach a footbridge and ford through the Wear. Do not cross this; rather, fork left on the lane, soon reaching the horse trough at **A** and bend left here back to the Market Place. ●

Armathwaite, Coombs Wood and Ainstable

		GPS waypoints
Start	Armathwaite, 9 miles (14.5km) south-east of Carlisle	

Start	Armathwaite, 9 miles (14.5km) south-east of Carlisle		NY 506 461
Distance	5½ miles (8.9km)	Ⓐ	NY 504 453
Height gain	640ft (195m)	Ⓑ	NY 517 444
Approximate time	3 hours	Ⓒ	NY 519 449
Parking	Roadside in Armathwaite	Ⓓ	NY 528 449
		Ⓔ	NY 531 462
Ordnance Survey maps	Landranger 86 (Haltwhistle & Brampton), Explorer OL5 (The English Lakes – North-eastern area)	Ⓕ	NY 516 468

Starting from Armathwaite, where a medieval pele tower guards the ancient crossing of the river Eden, this walk rises gently through Coombs Wood, where red squirrels mount a rearguard action against the American greys and deer graze dappled glades. Excellent views up the Eden Valley are a prelude to ever-better panoramas of the North Pennine fells and the distant giants of the northern Lake District as the walk threads along quiet lanes and through wildflower-rich pastures to Ainstable.

Take the road down beside the **Dukes Head Inn** and cross the River Eden. Look for a stile and steps on the left at the far (eastern) end of the bridge, use these and turn sharp-left to walk beneath the bridge. A wide path soon develops, parallel to the river and beneath some magnificent specimen trees. Remain on this for ½ mile (800m) to reach a path junction Ⓐ above the old mill weir, noting en route the pele tower (with a Georgian façade) on the opposite bank.

Turn back left up the path into the trees. At the next waymarked post in 50 yds, turn right to join a fence-side path within the woodland edge. In 200 yds climb the stile and walk up the wide, grassy track rising into the main body of Coombs Wood. Shortly, an arrangement

of carved and worked stone blocks form a sculpture, *Vista*, from which point there are magnificent views through the trees up the Eden's wooded, twisting valley. Remain on the widening forestry road and keep left at major forks, rising to reach a small car park beside a lane Ⓑ.

Turn left; then in 200 yds take the narrow lane, right, for Longdales. Excellent views along the flanks of the North Pennines draw the eye to Cross Fell, the highest point in England's backbone. Immediately beyond the last cottage, the lane deteriorates; here turn left on the fingerposted bridleway that passes to the right of the cottage. As this green lane crests, take the bridleway for Bascodyke on the right Ⓒ. This runs between fences to a gate into a walled farm lane that drops to

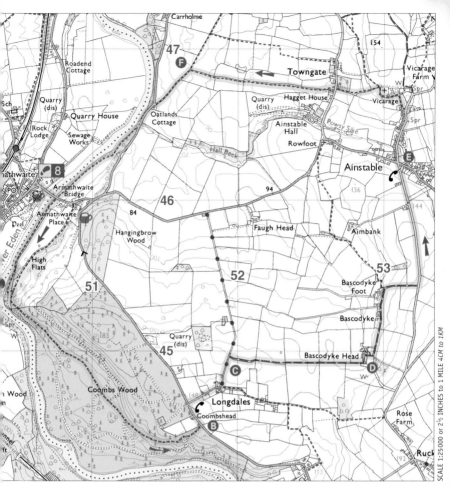

reach Bascodyke Head Farm. Turn left into the outer farmyard **D**.

Here, take the track on the right just past the first barn and walk up to the rough farm lane beyond and above the buildings. Turn left along this, which shortly becomes a tarred road, and walk past several other farms to reach a minor road. Turn left to Ainstable. At the crossroads **E** go straight ahead, cross the Powsy Sike beck and head uphill. In 250yds turn left to find hilltop St Michael & All Angels Church. Use the kissing-gate just past the lychgate and follow the wall round to another gate. Go through this and turn

left along the field edge; the path now passes through several stiles and gates to reach a lane.

Cross straight over into the entry, use a gate and walk the right-hand edge of the field to a stile. The focus of the immense views now shifts to the mountains of the northern Lake District, dominated by Blencathra and, breaking the northern horizon to your right, the mountains of Dumfries and Galloway in Scotland. Keep with the right-hand edge of a series of fields to a stile into a green lane **F**; here turn left towards Oatlands Cottage. Turn left down the lane and cross a bridge over Hall Beck. Here, turn right onto a riverside footpath back to Armathwaite. Cross the bridge to reach the village centre. ●

Durham – Riverside and Woods

Durham – Riverside and Woods

Start	Durham, Market Place		
Distance	4½ miles (7.2km)		
Height gain	215ft (65m)		
Approximate time	2½ hours		
Parking	Durham (Pay and Display)		
Ordnance Survey maps	Landranger 88 (Newcastle upon Tyne), Explorer 308 (Durham & Sunderland)		

GPS waypoints

🖉 NZ 273 425
Ⓐ NZ 278 425
Ⓑ NZ 284 416
Ⓒ NZ 276 402
Ⓓ NZ 274 407
Ⓔ NZ 274 415

Starting from the heart of Durham's medieval centre, this walk first drops to a riverside promenade beside the River Wear before joining a path through glorious broadleaf woodlands barely one mile from the city centre. Encountering tantalising evidence of long lost industry and a hill-fort, the walk passes the city's Botanic Garden before a final riverside flourish unveils unparalleled views of Durham's magnificent Cathedral and Castle which crown the top of the town within a tight loop of the Wear.

There are few grander sights in Britain than that of Durham Cathedral and Castle, side by side on a wooded cliff within a horseshoe bend in the River Wear. Together they symbolise the twin powers of the medieval bishops of Durham – military as well as spiritual – for they were prince bishops, entrusted by the king with the task of protecting the area from Scottish invasions. Clustered around these two mighty structures and enclosed within the loop of the river are narrow and winding streets, lined with gracious old buildings, many of them now housing various university departments, which give the city a distinctly medieval feel.

Durham Cathedral is a masterpiece of Norman architecture, widely regarded as the finest in Europe. Founded in 995 as the last resting-place of St Cuthbert, it was mostly constructed between 1093 and 1133, apart from the east end and central tower. Inside, the view is dominated by the majestic columns of the nave, characterised by the differing patterns on the stonework. The Galilee Chapel at the west end is the burial place of the Venerable Bede.

Although much altered and rebuilt by successive bishops, Durham Castle still retains the basic plan of the original Norman castle. The major alterations came after 1840 when it was given to the newly founded university and transformed into a residential college.

🖉 The walk starts in Durham's Market Place. Put your back to St Nicholas' Church tower porch and head half-left to pick up Saddler Street, beyond the statue of the Marquess of Londonderry on his horse. Fork left in

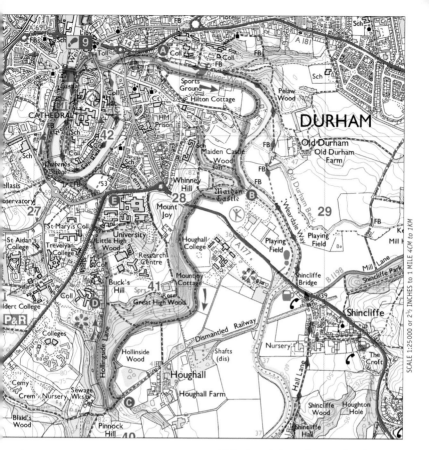

SCALE 1:25000 or 2½ INCHES to 1 MILE 4CM to 1KM

| 0 | 200 | 400 | 600 | 800 METRES | 1 |
| 0 | 200 | 400 | 600 YARDS | ½ | |

KILOMETRES
MILES

100 yds down the cobbled lane to find Elvet Bridge, one of the City's surviving medieval bridges. Use the near-end steps down to the left here and join the riverside promenade heading upstream beside the River Wear. Pass beneath a modern road bridge and continue beside the river to the modern Baths footbridge in a further 250 yds **A**.

Cross this and turn left, continuing upstream on the wide brick/tarred path between the river and the University Cricket Ground. This tranquil stretch ends at rowing club boathouses; use the gated track which loops right behind the compound here. Look diligently in 200 yds for the wide gap on your left at a barrier, at the near-end of the stand of larch trees, where National Cycle Route

70 is signed along the tarred path through the woodland edge. Follow this and turn left at the far side, shortly rejoining the riverside path at the abutments of an old railway bridge on the line to Durham Elvet Station (closed 1931). Advance upstream to approach the Maiden Castle footbridge beside the University boathouse **B**.

Don't cross the bridge; instead look right for the footpath within the woodland edge and follow this west around the foot of woods clothing the sharp hill of Maiden Castle, capped by an Iron Age promontory fort believed to date back 2,300 years. Stay left at the fork, remaining beside the playing fields to reach a main road. Carefully cross at the adjacent reservation and rejoin the woodland-foot path at the gateway. A magnificent ramble now ensues through the fringe of superb beech-woods which, in spring, have wonderful displays of ramsons, stitchwort and bluebells. Simply follow this path, in time passing beside wooden-palisade fencing. At the fork marked by a bench keep left, passing above an area of marshy pasture rich with birds. A board here notes that these woodlands of Great High and Hollinside have been in public ownership for over 170 years. The path presently reaches a T-junction at the top of an embankment **C**, the course of a colliery railway which closed in the 1880s.

Turn right and walk up intermittent steps to reach redundant gateposts on the course of a hard-surfaced track, Hollingside Lane. Turn right to rise gently up the ridge of Pinnock Hill, passing below a long series of robust stags-head oaks before reaching a

Durham Cathedral and old fulling mill

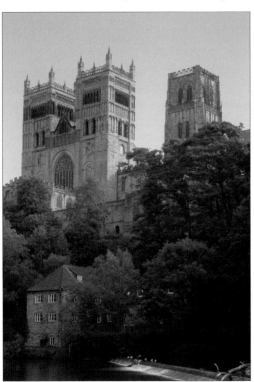

gateway into the university campus at old estate buildings. Walk ahead here on the now-tarred lane, passing by the entrance to the University Botanic Garden **D**. This attractive mix of theme gardens, research plots and sculptures is open most days (for a fee) to visitors. Stay with the roadway to reach a left-bend at the Victor Watts Library building (left). Here; turn right against the 'no entry' sign down the tarred lane beside Grey College hall of residence. At the next fork keep right, downhill to reach a bungalow. Take the tarred path right-of this and beside a tennis court; soon descend steps and then turn left to the main road. Cross at the lights and turn downhill to the major junction **E** in 250 yds.

Turn left along Quarry Heads Lane. Cross it immediately and look for the fingerposted footpath beside a bus shelter in 50 yds. Slip to the left beside the sports-field here and enter the strip of woodland. Keep downhill, shortly gaining a wide footpath which runs its course above the bank of the Wear. It's now a matter of continuing downstream, soon passing the end of Prebends Bridge. It's a memorable finalé to the walk, with Durham's Cathedral and Castle World Heritage Site looming high over the far bank above the sturdy old fulling mill, sited at the far end of the long weir.

At the next bridge - Framwellgate, Durham's oldest - climb the steps on your left, cross the bridge and ascend Silver Street to reach the nearby Market Place. ●

Causey Arch and Beamish Woods

		GPS waypoints
Start	Beamish Country Park off A6076, 4 miles (6.4km) south-west of Gateshead	🖉 NZ 204 561
		Ⓐ NZ 200 558
Distance	5 miles (8km)	Ⓑ NZ 195 551
Height gain	655ft (200m)	Ⓒ NZ 205 552
		Ⓓ NZ 204 546
Approximate time	2½ hours	Ⓔ NZ 215 542
Parking	Causey Arch Picnic Area	Ⓕ NZ 211 549
Ordnance Survey maps	Landranger 88 (Newcastle upon Tyne), Explorer 308 (Durham & Sunderland)	Ⓖ NZ 207 561

The walk takes you through a series of attractive woodlands, including the wooded gorge of Causey Burn, and there are many fine views over the surrounding countryside. The chief focal point and major historic site is the Causey Arch, one of the earliest engineering triumphs of the Industrial Revolution, which is said to be the oldest-surviving railway bridge in the world. The route also passes by the North of England Open Air Museum at Beamish, well worth a visit at the end of the walk.

🖉 Start next to the car park exit over-bridge by taking the signed path for Causey Arch, putting the railway embankment on the left. On reaching steps, turn right, in the 'Causey Arch via Gorge' direction, and descend into the gorge. Do not cross the first footbridge over Causey Burn but turn left alongside the burn and cross it at the second footbridge.

Continue through the wooded gorge, turn left over the next footbridge to recross the burn, climb steps, turn right and at the next bend Causey Arch is seen ahead. Cross the burn again, turn left to the arch, turn sharp right to climb steps beside it and turn left up to a T-junction Ⓐ.

Divert to the left over the arch, both to enjoy the fine view and to see a replica wooden waggon and short length of wooden track on the other side. Causey Arch was built between 1725 and '26 to carry the wooden railway track across the gorge of the Causey Burn and is the oldest-surviving single-arch railway bridge in the world. The railway was constructed to carry coal from local mines to the River Tyne, but after an explosion at the nearby Tanfield Colliery in 1740 coal production declined and the waggonway across the arch closed in 1786. Iron rails and steam locomotives were later used on a new route but this closed in 1962. Part of that line is now used by a private company.

Return to the T-junction and keep

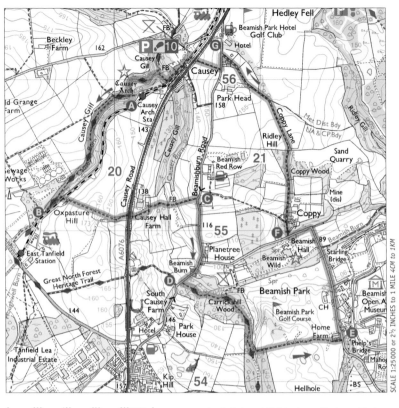

SCALE 1:25,000 or 2½ INCHES to 1 MILE 4CM to 1KM

```
0    200   400   600  800 METRES  1
                                    KILOMETRES
                                    MILES
0    200   400   600 YARDS   ½
```

ahead through the woods. At the fork, keep left at the sign for 'Top of Causey Gorge' and join a ledged route high above the burn. This descends very gradually; after ¾ mile (1.2km) use the footbridge on your left **B** and turn left off the far end. Walk with the path as it rises out of the valley and the woods to a waymarked post. Turn sharp right here, cross the Tanfield Railway via gates and climb steps at the far side, curling with the path round to a stile. Head uphill along the left edge of the field, go through a fence gap at the crest and continue down the wide path through immature woodland. At the slope foot turn left on the grassy track to reach the main road.

Cross over, descend steps, turn right along a narrow path and turn left over a stile. Bear slightly left to walk along the left-hand field edge, climb a stile in the corner, turn left and head down to reach a gap between a wall and a hedge. Fork right here, dropping beside the woodland edge before entering the woods and descending steps to reach and cross a footbridge beyond a grassy clearing. Keep left at the fork to use a stile below electricity cables and then walk steeply uphill with a holly hedge on your right. At the corner climb a stile into a lane **C**.

Turn downhill and follow the lane to and over Beamish Burn. About 200 yds beyond this, use the open archway (just above a track and barrier) through the estate wall on your left **D** and go ahead into the woods. Fork right along the wider track in 30 paces, following this over a culvert and then gradually right and gently uphill through the woods. At a T-junction about 250 yds past a wooden barrier turn left; in a further 100 yds fork left on the track which rises beside the parkland wall, shortly using a gap-stile onto Beamish Park Golf Course. Walk straight ahead past the eighth tee and then along a line of silver birch, keeping ahead on the grassy road towards the buildings. Immediately before reaching these, look slightly right for a sign on the wall 'Exit from Public Footpath.' Climb the steps through the wall to enter the yard of the estate forge; use the gate on your right and turn left to walk through the period farmyard here at Beamish Home Farm.

Turn left along the lane **E**. On the right are the grounds of the North of England Open Air Museum at Beamish, a revealing and imaginative recreation of life in the North at the turn of the century. There is a lot to see and do here – farm, trams, railway station, coal mine and colliery village – and a visit is recommended at the end of the walk.

Head downhill along the lane, crossing a bridge over Beamish Burn and passing the entrance to Beamish Hall, and follow the lane around a left bend. At a public footpath sign to Causey Arch, turn right **F** onto a broad track (Coppy Lane) that heads steadily uphill and enters Coppy Wood. Pass beside a gate to leave the woods along a rough track between fields; this bends left at a copse to reach the entrance to a farm storage complex. At this point fork right along the narrower path, shortly emerging onto a drive that drops to a road **G**. **The Causey Arch Inn** is 150 yds to the right here.

Turn left and, at a public footpath sign, turn right over a stile and head gently downhill along the left edge of a field. Climb a stile in the bottom corner and turn left down to a road. Cross over and take the tarmac path opposite, passing under a railway bridge, to the car park. ●

Causey Arch

Hamsterley Forest

		GPS waypoints
Start	Hamsterley Forest Visitor Centre, near Hamsterley, 10 miles (16km) west of Bishop Auckland	🖉 NZ 091 312
		Ⓐ NZ 086 308
Distance	5 miles (8km)	Ⓑ NZ 084 304
Height gain	670ft (205m)	Ⓒ NZ 079 299
Approximate time	2½ hours	Ⓓ NZ 066 299
		Ⓔ NZ 068 309
Parking	Forest Visitor Centre (toll road, fee payable)	Ⓕ NZ 071 312
Ordnance Survey maps	Landranger 92 (Barnard Castle), Explorer OL31 (North Pennines – Teesdale & Weardale)	

This walk is essentially a circuit around both sides of the valley of Bedburn Beck, an undulating route with several ascents and descents that takes you beside sparkling becks and through mixed woodland, with some fine views over the forest from the higher points. The route is an engaging mix of forest tracks and rides, byways and winding forest paths with great spring wildflowers and autumn colours.

Hamsterley Forest, the largest in County Durham, comprises over 4,800 acres (2,000 ha) of mixed woodlands. It was formerly a hunting estate and was purchased by the Forestry Commission in 1927 when the original conifer plantings were begun.

🖉 Put your back to the Visitor Centre and take the ramped path, half-right, then cross the nearby steel-arched wooden bridge across Bedburn Beck. Turn right along the wide path past keep-fit equipment to reach a T-junction beside the Pooh Stick Bridge. Turn left up the wider forest track to reach a higher T-junction Ⓐ. Turn left (orange waymark arrow) and walk 100 yds to another orange waymarked post. Here, turn right up the narrow woodland path and rise quite steeply to reach a wide forestry road. Turn right and advance to the angled crossing of a tarred lane just past a barrier Ⓑ. Cross

diagonally, joining another gravelly forest track that rises through an area of felled woods now bright with gorse. The track presently re-enters woodland before bending left to continue uphill. It gradually thins to a path before reaching a tarred road Ⓒ.

Turn right along this. It's a peaceful back road which soon reveals excellent views to your right, across to the high moorland ridge above Weardale and the distinct quiff of the Elephant Trees on the horizon. In 750 yds turn right at the footpath fingerpost (opposite a lane junction) and join the thin, steep path down through the plantation woods, shortly dappled with broadleaf trees. At the foot of decrepit wooden steps you'll reach a forestry road.

Cross diagonally-left to rejoin the waymarked orange route path; cross a lower tarred lane before dropping further to find another tarred road. Turn left on the path closely parallel to this and then cross the nearby new road bridge over Bedburn Beck. Take the track immediately to the right, which curls gradually left to reach the near-end of a footbridge .

Don't cross this; instead continue on the narrow tarred lane which bends right and starts steadily uphill. Remain with this past the remote house on your left in 500 yds. The track roughens a little; to the right are grand views across the heart of Hamsterley Forest. Ignore the next left-turn. The woods-edge way levels before reaching a point where another roadway comes in from your left, separated by a line of boulders **E**.

Cross into the other roadway momentarily, then turn right (orange arrow) onto the narrow path within the trees, avoiding the deeply rutted, muddy track now used by mountain bikers. At the slope-foot bear right a few paces before crossing the footbridge over Ayhope Beck to reach the ruins of Metcalf's coaching inn **F**.

In Hamsterley Forest

Turn right on the signed path behind this and walk the pleasing woodland path above the beck to reach a green where the 'Green Man' totem-pole sculpture stands. Turn right on the lane here, cross the nearby river bridge and turn left into the rough Low Redford car park. Take the surfaced path from the back-left of this; re-cross the beck and remain on this path past fenced meadows renowned for spring cowslips. The path briefly rejoins a tarred lane before drifting right again into the woods. Upon reaching the near-end of Pooh Stick Bridge, walk ahead beside the beck and past the adventure playground to find the Visitor Centre. ●

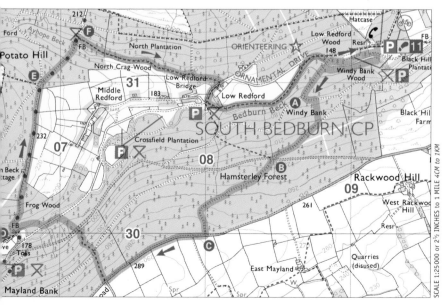

Around Dufton Pike

		GPS waypoints
Start	Dufton, 3 miles (4.8km) north of Appleby-in-Westmorland	🖊 NY 689 249
Distance	5 miles (8km)	Ⓐ NY 685 253
Height gain	625ft (190m)	Ⓑ NY 681 269
Approximate time	2½ hours	Ⓒ NY 692 273
Parking	Dufton village car park	Ⓓ NY 704 267
Ordnance Survey maps	Landranger 91 (Appleby-in-Westmorland), Explorer OL19 (Howgill Fells & Upper Eden Valley)	

Dufton Pike is the prominent, conically shaped hill (1,578ft/ 481m) north of Dufton. After a brief opening stretch through the steep-sided, wooded Dufton Ghyll or Gill, the route becomes a circuit of the lower slopes of the Pike, providing both pleasant and relatively easy walking and a succession of outstanding views of the surrounding, loftier peaks of the North Pennines. On the final leg – a gradual descent – the views extend across the gentler terrain of the Eden valley to the line of the Lakeland fells.

The attractive village of Dufton lies between two of the wildest, loneliest and most challenging stretches of the Pennine Way. Its pub, farms and red sandstone cottages, grouped around a wide green with a Victorian drinking-fountain, are overlooked by Dufton Pike.

🖊 Turn right from the car park and immediately right again along a gravelled road with a fingerpost for Dufton Ghyll. Walk this fenced way between caravan and camping fields before descending left into the wooded gorge. Turn sharp right with the hairpin bend across the beck and slowly regain height on the track along the south side of the Ghyll. In a further 150 yds fork right at a fingerpost for Mill Bridge; at a cross path keep ahead on a path beneath cherry and birch trees. Cross a footbridge and trace the path through to a hand-gate into a lane. Turn left, cross the bridge over Mill Beck and walk a

further 50 paces to a stile on the right Ⓐ.

Climb this (signed for Church Bridge) and walk beside the wire fence on the left, then keep ahead to an offset woodland corner and waymarked stile. Enter the woods here and walk along the bottom inside edge, use a stile and carry on to cross a slab bridge over a side beck. Use the gate here and continue with the beck on your right, shortly reaching a lane at Church Bridge. St Cuthbert's Church is concealed in trees ahead; your route is to the left along the minor road, remaining on this to reach the picturesque hamlet of Knock Ⓑ.

At the sharp left bend into the near-end of the village's main street, jig right and then immediately left at a fingerpost for Knock Fell and Dufton. Walk through the farmyard (barn on your left), continuing then along a walled track with the radar dome on

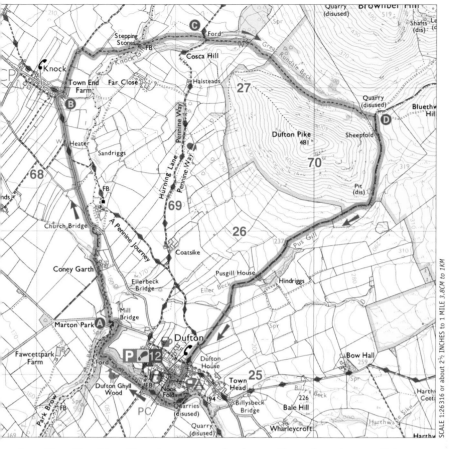

| 0 | 200 | 400 | 600 | 800 METRES | 1 |
| 0 | 200 | 400 | 600 YARDS | ½ | KILOMETRES / MILES |

Great Dun Fell straight ahead and Dufton Pike off to your right. Keep right at a fork to reach a fingerpost 'Dufton via Back of Pike.' Climb the stile and walk the right edge of the field; join the walled track and bend left along this, rising to a stile on the right 100 yds before the end of this track. Climb this, walk the left edge of the field to another stile near the corner and climb this.

Walk ahead beside the line of an old hedge bank to gain a waymarked, offset wall corner: from this point fork right to find a path down into Knock Gill and cross the footbridge. Use the adjacent stile and rise through the trees to a second stile, once over which walk ahead across the reedy pasture, parallel to Great Rundale Beck down to your right. Pass through a derelict wall and walk on to the far end of the pasture and climb a stile.

Turn right, cross the clapper bridge ⒞ and use another stile, here turning left along a rutted track that starts to curl around the foot of Dufton Pike. Remain with this track, cross a couple of stone stiles and rise very gradually across the Pike's flank, superb views up the dramatic gash cut by Great Rundale Beck soon opening out to your left. The grassy track eventually reaches a tall gate into an old quarry road ⒟. Turn right along this, remaining with the wide, rough old track through a series of gates to return to Dufton. Walk ahead on the lane and bend right to return to the car park. ●

Kirkby Stephen and Nateby

		GPS waypoints
Start	Kirkby Stephen	 NY 775 087
Distance	6½ miles (10.5km)	Ⓐ NY 778 086
Height gain	475ft (145m)	Ⓑ NY 774 066
Approximate time	3½ hours	Ⓒ NY 768 066
Parking	Main car park off Silver Street, Kirkby Stephen	Ⓓ NY 757 062
		Ⓔ NY 748 071
Ordnance Survey maps	Landranger 91 (Appleby-in-Westmorland), Explorer OL19 (Howgill Fells & Upper Eden Valley)	Ⓕ NY 764 077

After an attractive opening stretch beside the River Eden, the route continues into the village of Nateby and then heads gently uphill out of the valley, giving fine views of the North Pennines and Howgill Fells. The last 2 miles (3.2km) are on the Coast to Coast Path – a gradual descent into Kirkby Stephen with views of the town nestling below in the Eden valley. All the climbs on this walk are gradual and relatively easy.

Kirkby Stephen is a long, narrow town situated on the west bank of the River Eden. The hub of the town is the Market Square, where the walk begins.

 With your back to the Butter Market and medieval church – the latter is one of the largest and grandest in Cumbria – turn left along Stoneshot, following signs to River Eden and Frank's Bridge. Continue along a tarmac path between high walls that bends right and, at another sign to River Eden and Frank's Bridge, turn left down steps and cross the nearby bridge over the Eden. Turn right along the firm path above the river.

Go through a kissing-gate and, within a few paces, bear right at a fingerpost for Pod Gill Ⓐ, tracing a route close to the riverside fence. In the corner beyond the stone barn, use a hand-gate, cross a footbridge over a side stream and follow the path right, through the neck of

woodland. Beyond the trees, the route becomes a narrow way between fencing and overhanging bushes. In ⅓ mile cross a footbridge over a brook and follow the wide, sunken path ahead, rising to cross a bridge over a disused railway. Bear right, but remain on the enclosed field side track *(do not join the railway path)*; at a fork bear right, cross a slab bridge and rise to the road. Walk ahead through Nateby, passing the village green (left) and pub (right).

Just before the compound on the right, take the footpath for Wharton Hall, over a stone stile  and along a ginnel to and through a metal hand-gate. Walk straight ahead across the pasture, use a field gate through the fence and head slightly left to a hand-gate, from which drop to the riverside at a kissing-gate. Walk upstream, cross the tractor bridge and climb the sloping field to use a gate into a concreted road. Turn right and descend to the strip of trees **C**.

Turn left up the gated track immediately beyond these. Use the next gate and bear left in 75 yds on a side-track below cables. Advance through the dip up to the shallow-angled fenced corner (on your left), just round which use the waymarked stile and turn right beside the fence. Bear right at the next

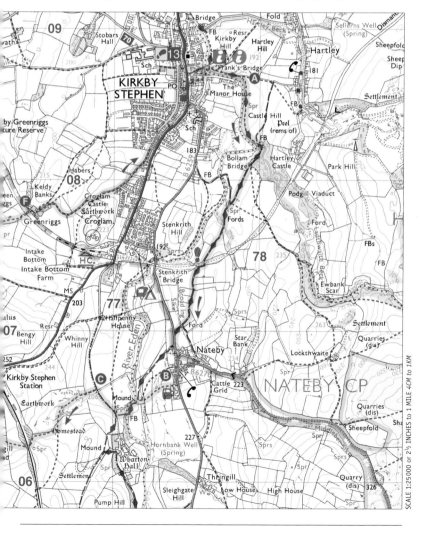

SCALE 1:25000 or 2½ INCHES to 1 MILE 4CM to 1KM

corner and head up to the bridge arch visible below the railway. Use it and drift right towards farm buildings, go through a gate and then half-right to use another one. Turn left and walk to the farm complex. Use the gate into the farmyard, turn left in front of the farmhouse and then right beyond a stone barn; then follow the access drive to a main road. Turn right to a busy junction ⓓ.

Carefully cross the A685 and turn left along the wide verge. In 150 yds turn right along the lane signed for Waitby and Smardale. After $^3/_4$ mile (1.2km) take the first turn on the right ⓔ and walk downhill for 200 yds to find a fingerpost on the right, signed Kirkby Lonsdale and Coast to Coast Path. Head diagonally downhill across a field towards a wall on the far side, bear right alongside the wall and, at a corner, turn left and keep ahead to pass under a railway bridge again. Keep ahead across the next field, bearing

gradually right to climb a stone stile in the far corner.

Now bear slightly left and, as you head downhill, a grand view opens up over the Eden valley with the tower of Kirkby Stephen church visible. After climbing a stile, continue through a shallow valley down to a stone stile, climb it, walk along the right-hand field edge, go through a gate and pass between the supports of a former railway bridge to a metal gate ⓕ. Turn right in front of a barn, go through another metal gate and turn left between farm buildings.

Follow the winding farm access road to reach the outskirts of Kirkby Stephen. Bear left at a junction, keeping housing on your right. The lane is intermittently tarred or rough; presently it passes garages and becomes a tarred road parallel to the main street. At a footpath sign on the left for 'Car Park', turn right along the ginnel to return to the Market Square (or left to the car park). ●

Mallerstang Edge

Sunbiggin Tarn and Great Asby Scar

		GPS waypoints
Start	Sunbiggin Tarn, 5 miles (8km) north-east of Junction 38 of the M6	🖉 NY 675 078
		Ⓐ NY 668 096
Distance	6¾ miles (10.9km)	Ⓑ NY 644 099
Height gain	510ft (155m)	Ⓒ NY 640 097
		Ⓓ NY 639 082
Approximate time	3½ hours	Ⓔ NY 653 082
Parking	Roadside near cattle-grid at Sunbiggin Tarn	Ⓕ NY 669 082
Ordnance Survey maps	Landranger 91 (Appleby-in-Westmorland), Explorer OL19 (Howgill Fells & Upper Eden Valley)	

Sunbiggin Tarn glints like a jewel in the great bowl of heathery moorland separating the stately Howgill Fells from the undulating plateau between the rivers Lune and Eden. The area is noted for its bounty of wild bird species and rare lime-loving plants. Paths rise easily to Great Asby Scar, a rare and fantastical landscape of limestone pavement dappled with Neolithic settlement remains and offering enormous views. The return leg passes an evocative stone circle dating from the same mists of time.

Walking across limestone pavement requires that particular care be taken, as there are deep fissures and loose slabs to contend with. We recommend that you do not follow this route when snow covers the ground.

🖉 With the cattle-grid behind you and the Tarn to your left, walk along the road for 200 yds to a bridleway fingerpost on your right. Turn along the track here, remaining on this as it starts to rise towards the distant limestone crags. At a cross-tracks, keep ahead through an area of gnarled hawthorn trees to use a gate through a wall and continue gradually uphill, to a wall on your left. Go through a second gate and remain beside the wall, presently reaching the first of many limestone

exposures. Near a walled corner, use the bridlegate and walk slightly left across the grassy area to reach a low waymark post Ⓐ.

Turn left to another nearby waymark post. Here the bridleway turns right, but you keep ahead along a sheep track, paralleling the wall on your left. Drift gradually towards this, meeting it at a ladder-stile and fence. Climb the stile and keep the wall on your left. The route rises gently onto the ever-spreading limestone plateau of Great Asby Scar National Nature Reserve (NNR). The remarkable pavement of clints (upstanding blocks) and grikes (deep fissures) has formed over thousands of years by the action of groundwater, frost and snow. Look into the grikes,

Limestone pavement on Great Asby Scar

a wall on your right. Follow this through to a gated corner just below a small, capped reservoir. Use two gates and walk the rough lane for 200 yds to a fingerpost on the left  (Bridleway to Acres and Coast to Coast path to Sunbiggin). This is your route, but take a short detour ahead to see the Gamelands Stone Circle on the left. There is no public access, but the 33 stones are easily viewed.

Return to the fingerpost (now on your right), climb the stile and walk towards the distant stone barn, a wall on your right, then on the left after a bridlegate. Beyond the barn, a long series of stone stiles brings you to a lane at Acres which are veritable miniature gorges of ferns and wildflowers. Extraordinary views open all around, from the Howgills in the south to the Lake District and Blencathra in the west and up and down the Pennines to the east.

Use a bridlegate through a cross-fence and continue beside the wall. About 550 yds past here, the trig pillar on distant Knott comes into view; here, turn right and pick a way across the pavement to a raised grassy area bounded by tumbled blocks and cairns. This was the fortified Neolithic settlement of Castle Folds and encloses the remains of stone huts. From here sight the trig pillar, walk towards it and climb the ladder-stile at the walled corner. With a wall on your left (and the trig pillar beyond), gradually descend from the plateau (the path is awkward underfoot) into a narrow pass through the limestone pavement, marked by an NNR board ⓑ.

Turn left through the bridlegate and walk the springy turf path, a wall gradually coming closer from your left. Use the bridlegate through this wall ⓒ and join another grassy track which shortly bends right and runs just above

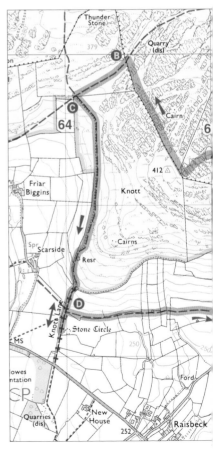

Sunbiggin Tarn

Cottage **E**. Turn left and walk the tarred lane to its end just above Stony Head Farm. Here fork right along the walled bridleway for Sunbiggin Tarn. Beyond a gate, keep ahead on the rough road to a crossing of tracks and an Access Land board **F**. Turn right here, keep left at a fork and follow the grassy track to another Access Land board. Go straight over the cross-ways here and walk the track through to the cattle-grid above the Tarn. ●

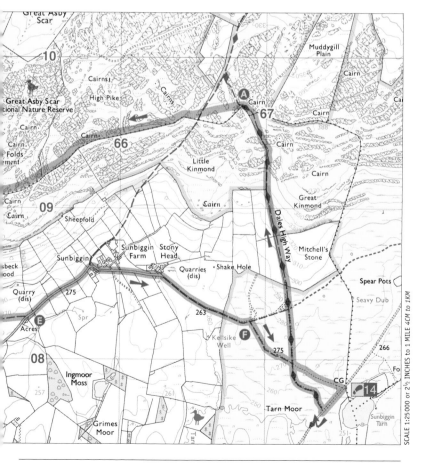

Marsden Rock and Whitburn

		GPS waypoints	
Start	Marsden Bay, South Shields, just south of the junction of the A183 (Coast Road) and the A1300 (Redwell Lane)	🖉	NZ 397 650
		Ⓐ	NZ 400 647
		Ⓑ	NZ 390 640
Distance	7 miles (11.3km)	Ⓒ	NZ 388 633
Height gain	375ft (115m)	Ⓓ	NZ 403 623
		Ⓔ	NZ 404 617
Approximate time	3½ hours	Ⓕ	NZ 407 612
Parking	Marsden Bay, car park (Pay and Display)	Ⓖ	NZ 414 627
Ordnance Survey maps	Landranger 88 (Newcastle upon Tyne), Explorer 316 (Newcastle upon Tyne)		

Initially the walk heads inland, climbing gently over the modest Cleadon Hills (272ft/83m) and then descending to the attractive coastal village of Whitburn. From here the rest of the route hugs the coast, keeping along the top of low cliffs and passing several stacks and rock arches. Because of the instability of the cliffs, it is important not to cross the barrier while walking along the coast path.

🖉 Begin by heading across the grass to the coast path and turn right along it to the huge limestone stack of Marsden Rock, renowned for its seabird colonies. Until recently it was the most impressive arch on this stretch of coast but the arch collapsed a few years ago in a storm.

From the rock, bear right back to the road, cross it and, at a public bridleway sign to the left of a caravan park, join the enclosed path Ⓐ which winds gently uphill between the caravan park and a golf course to reach a lane. Turn left; then within a few paces go right along the bridleway signed for Cleadon Park. This rises past houses on your left and the grassy old Marsden Quarry on your right. Views on a clear day stretch across the Tyne Estuary and Newcastle to the

distant, shadowy profile of the Cheviot Hills in northern Northumberland. Keep beside a combination of hedge, fence and wall on your left to reach a signboard for 'Marsden Old Quarry Local Nature Reserve.'

Use the stile Ⓑ through the wall on your left here and walk across the golf course, guided by yellow posts, in-line just left of the brick tower (a water pumping station). At the far side of the fairways enter an area of dog roses along a red-gravelled path. In three paces fork left along a narrower path to reach a high metal kissing-gate, go through this and keep the wall on your left. Cross a farm track to reach a kissing-gate Ⓒ just beyond an unusual sculpted seat. Use this and walk beside the wall to and past the gaunt stone

tower of Cleadon Windmill; views to
the south encompass Sunderland,
Wearmouth and the Cleveland Hills.

At the walled corner fork half-left
across the grassed area; shortly keep left
at a fork to go over a wooden stile
through rail fencing marked with a

'Bedes Way' disc. Wind with the path
along the right edge of the field formed
by a very low cliff. At the far corner go
through a stile into a narrow, fenced

Whitburn Bay and Roker Pier Light

Carroll's famous poem *The Walrus and the Carpenter;* the author visited cousins who lived in Whitburn.

Cross left into Sea Lane and walk past the seafood café to reach a large car park. Look right for the waymarked coastal footpath and join this along the grassy downs backing the low cliffs here. It's now a matter of ambling along the cliff-top path northwards, passing through several gates which marked the boundary of the former Whitburn Rifle Ranges. The grassy old rifle butts crowd above the rocky bays here.

Above Souter Point **G**, the crescent beach of Jackie's Bay marks the place where the cliffs become more prominent and the memorable stacks, pillars and bluffs of Marsden Bay take the eye. Don't fail to look south, though, for a grand view down the coast to the curving breakwaters which protect the docks and harbours at Wearmouth, marked by the Roker Pier Light.

Now comes the most spectacular part of the coast walk as the path keeps by a wall on the left bordering the Whitburn Coastal Park, an area of grassland reclaimed from the site of the former Whitburn Colliery. Part of it is a nature reserve. Ahead are Souter Lighthouse and Lizard Point and on this stretch of coast there are several stacks and rock arches. Pass beside a barrier to the right of the lighthouse, built in 1871 and now open to the public, and continue across The Leas, a National Trust area of grassland, cliffs and beaches. On the other side of the road are the imposing remains of the 19th-century Marsden Limekilns.

Continue along the coast path to Marsden Rock and on to the start. ●

path that shortly becomes a causeway between fields; bend left, then right, use a step stile into an enclosed path, use a further stile and turn left along the left edge of a field to walk to the distant farm. Climb the stile into the farmyard complex and walk ahead, barns on your left, through to a road at the edge of Whitburn **D**.

Turn right, at a T-junction turn right again, take the first turning on the left – Sandy Chare – and at the next junction turn left again **E** along Whitburn's attractive village green, lined by handsome 18th- and 19th-century houses. Bear right along a tarmac path across a corner of the green, turn right along Church Lane, passing the mainly 13th-century church, and where the lane ends keep ahead beside a barrier and continue along an enclosed tarmac track, beside a park on the left. You reach the coast road **F** at The Bents, marking the northern end of the superb beach of Whitburn Bay. This is said to have been an inspiration for Lewis

Auckland Park, Escomb and the River Wear

		GPS waypoints	
Start	Bishop Auckland Market Place	🖊	NZ 211 301
Distance	7½ miles (12.1km) Two shorter versions of 3 miles (5.6km) and 4½ miles (6.4km)	Ⓐ	NZ 214 299
		Ⓑ	NZ 227 302
		Ⓒ	NZ 225 310
Height gain	625ft (190m)	Ⓓ	NZ 211 303
Approximate time	3½ hours (2 hours for Escomb loop; 1½ for Park loop)	Ⓔ	NZ 205 301
		Ⓕ	NZ 199 294
Parking	Bishop Auckland (Pay and Display)	Ⓖ	NZ 189 301
		Ⓗ	NZ 190 291
Ordnance Survey maps	Landrangers 92 (Barnard Castle) and 93 (Middlesbrough), Explorer 305 (Bishop Auckland)	Ⓙ	NZ 194 290
		Ⓚ	NZ 197 293

There is considerable historic interest on this figure-of-eight walk, centred on the town of Bishop Auckland. The first half is essentially a circuit of the boundary of Auckland Park, once the deer park of Auckland Castle, the palace of the bishops of Durham. The second half takes you along the banks of the River Wear, under a massive Victorian viaduct and across delightful meadows, to the little Saxon church at Escomb. The route can obviously be split into two separate, shorter walks. On the second part of the walk, there is one short, muddy and uneven section.

The large Market Place in Bishop Auckland is dominated by the handsome Victorian town hall, built in 1862, and adjoining it is the almost contemporary St Anne's Church. Leading off from the Market Place is the 18th-century gatehouse to Auckland Castle, since the 12th century the seat of the powerful Prince Bishops of Durham. Although much altered and restored, the castle has some interesting features and is particularly noted for the magnificent chapel, converted from a medieval, aisled hall in the 17th century.

🖊 The full walk and both the shorter alternatives start in the Market Place, in front of the town hall.

If doing the second part of the walk only – along the river to Escomb – pass to the left of the town hall, take the first turning on the left and descend steeply to the river, joining the full walk at point Ⓓ.

For the first part of the walk only – the circuit of Auckland Park – and the full walk, pass to the right of the town hall, by St Anne's Church, and turn right in front of the entrance to Auckland Castle. Bear left at the junction ahead, in the Spennymoor and Durham direction; just after a road comes in from the right, look carefully on your left for a

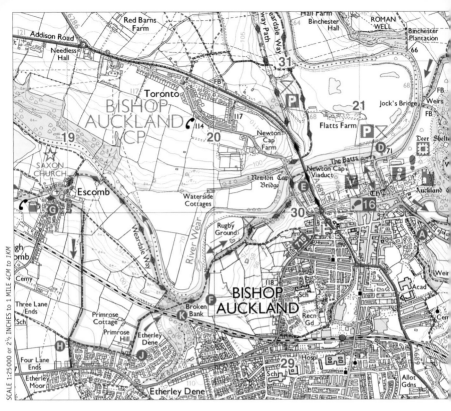

public footpath sign indicating narrow steps up to a stile Ⓐ. Climb it and take the path ahead to climb another one.

Head uphill by the left-hand edge of a field, alongside the boundary wall of Auckland Park – part of which is now Bishop Auckland golf course – and climb a stile in the top corner. Cross the drive leading to the golf club, keep ahead along an enclosed path, climb a stile and continue along the left-hand edge of three fields, climbing two more stiles. After climbing another stile in the bottom corner of the third field, turn left Ⓑ onto a straight, flat and well-surfaced track. This was formerly part of the railway line between Bishop Auckland and Spennymoor.

At first the track runs along the top of a low embankment and then continues through a wooded cutting. After passing under the first bridge, turn right up steps, turn left at the top, climb a stile and turn left to cross the second bridge

Ⓒ. Walk along a left-hand field edge and continue along the left-hand edge of a succession of fields and over a series of stiles, with the deer park over to the left, finally bearing left to climb a stile onto a lane. Bear left alongside the River Wear, cross a bridge over the little River Gaunless by its confluence with the Wear and continue along the lane to where it turns left Ⓓ. Ahead are fine views of Newton Cap Viaduct, and Auckland Castle can be seen on the hill to the left.

If only doing the circuit of Auckland Park, turn left and follow the lane steeply uphill to the start.

For the full walk, turn right along a tarmac drive, follow it around a left-hand bend and, where it ends, keep ahead across riverside meadows, passing under the viaduct. The imposing Newton Cap Viaduct was constructed between 1856 and '57 to carry the railway over the River Wear. It was closed

| 0 | 200 | 400 | 600 | 800 METRES | 1 |
| 0 | 200 | 400 | 600 YARDS | ½ | |

KILOMETRES
MILES

in 1968 and has subsequently been converted into a road bridge. Continue to a bridge, climb steps in front of it up to a road, turn left uphill and take the first turning on the right **E**, signed as the Weardale Way and to Bishop Auckland Rugby Club. Follow the tarred lane past the rugby club to its end at a small car park.

Use the stile into the meadow and walk upstream for about 150 yds to the point where gorse prevents further progress. Here turn left uphill at a Weardale Way waymarked post, in 75 yds turn right at another waymarked post along a path into the undergrowth **F**. This path – which may be muddy – undulates through the scrub, crossing a section of boardwalk (keep right shortly after this) to a fork. Bear right, go through the kissing-gate and wind with the path, keeping an eye out for a footbridge on your right. Cross this and turn left on a riverside path beside the Wear. The route passes through several redundant stiles before becoming a

fenced path above the river, at the end of which stretch is a kissing-gate. Use this and turn left on the dirt path to reach a small fenced compound and a gate into a tarred lane. Walk up past the houses to a junction and turn left; Escomb church **G** is on your right in its circular, tree-shaded churchyard.

St. John's dates from the 7th century and is one of England's small handful of surviving Saxon churches, partially built from stone robbed from the nearby Roman fort of Vinovia (Binchester). Make time to explore this magnificent part of England's heritage; if locked, the keys are available nearby.

With your back to the churchyard gateway, look left to locate Bede Close and walk along this. In 50 paces keep left along a tarred footpath in front of bungalows. Use the hand-gate into an enclosed path; at the far end climb the stile and fork right up a bridleway, a wood-rail fence on your left. Rise on this wide, occasionally fenced bridleway along the right of pastures, using gates/stiles as appropriate to reach and cross a railway bridge. At the top corner **H** go through a kissing-gate and turn sharp-left on a tarred path alongside the foot of houses' gardens. At the far end, go through a kissing-gate and walk ahead on the gravel path to a lane **J**.

Turn left and walk in front of the row of cottages. As the rough lane turns left, keep ahead on a narrowing track past a brick building and climb a stile beside a gate. The path drops to cross an overgrown railway; climb the stile beyond the track and turn right onto a path that drops into the scrubby wood-land. Trace this down Broken Bank to a T-junction **K**; turn right here, rejoining your outward route. Cross the boardwalk and retrace the walk back to **D**. Here, turn right up the steep lane to return to the Market Place. ●

Egglestone Abbey, Paradise and the Meeting of the Waters

Start	Egglestone Abbey, 1½ miles (2.4km) south-east of Barnard Castle
Distance	7 miles (11.3km)
Height gain	215ft (65m)
Approximate time	3 hours
Parking	Egglestone Abbey
Ordnance Survey maps	Landranger 92 (Barnard Castle), Explorer OL31 (North Pennines – Teesdale & Weardale)

GPS waypoints

- 🖊 NZ 062 150
- Ⓐ NZ 065 149
- Ⓑ NZ 079 142
- Ⓒ NZ 084 144
- Ⓓ NZ 086 142
- Ⓔ NZ 106 146
- Ⓕ NZ 084 146

This is a straightforward walk beside the River Tees as it flows majestically by crags and rocks through woodland and farmland. There are monastic ruins, an ancient tower and a grand country-house along the route, and on every inch of the path you are treading in the footsteps of great painters and writers from the Romantic age.

🖊 Leave the car park at Egglestone Abbey and head back down the access road beside the ruins. The abbey was built in a charming position over-looking the Tees, where it is joined by the waters of the Thorsgill Beck. It was a Premonstratensian foundation of the late 12th century, colonised by the monks

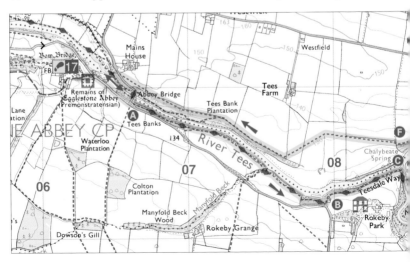

from Easby Abbey, near Richmond. After the dissolution it was converted into a manor house, but enough of its fabric survives to make this still a holy spot.

Bear right along Abbey Lane to reach the bridge **A**. Cross diagonally over the road (but not the bridge) and take the sloping path signed as the Teesdale Way which curls down into the woods to join a secluded path through the shallow limestone gorge. The River Tees swirls, pools and cataracts beneath fractured wooded crags and buttresses; the path leaves its waterside route at Manyfold Beck and rises steeply to pastures at the woodland edge. Remain beside this woodland to use a stile to enter Paradise – a spinney of elegant broadleaf trees with a rich variety of lime-loving plants – and wind with the path to reach a stile at a road junction **B**.

Turn left along the 'No Through Road' – Mortham Lane – to walk between the strand of riverside trees and the parkland pastures surrounding Rokeby Park. This country house was built in 1730 by Sir Thomas Robinson, who was a noted amateur architect and patron of the arts. Sir Walter Scott stayed here on working holidays to write his novels and poetry, and the painters Turner and Cotman recorded all of Teesdale's beauty spots while based at Rokeby. One of Turner's greatest landscapes is of the *Meeting of the Waters*, where the turbulent Greta joins the broader Tees **C**. This scene remained unchanged from Turner's visit until the floods caused by the hurricane in October 1987 rearranged the bedrock in an awesome demonstration of elemental force.

Walk around to the lodge house and turn left to cross Dairy Bridge, a spectacular leap over the limestone gorge of the River Greta. Remain on the driveway and rise gradually around the bend to a point **D** some 100 yds before the gate into the grounds of Mortham Tower, an eye-catching building created from a 14th century pele tower built as refuge from border raiders. Turn left at the stand of young trees (waymark disc here) and walk to a stone step-stile to the left of a gate. Enter the pasture and walk along its top edge. A grassy hedgeside path develops along the lip of a ridge; to the left, overgrown medieval cultivation terraces drop towards the Tees and newly planted copses dot the estate. Here and there you'll notice

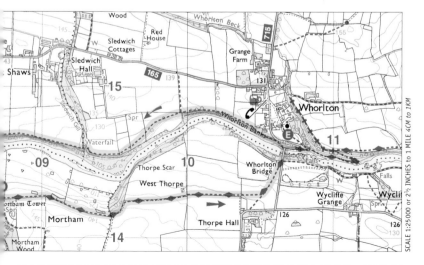

large, globular boulders beside the path; these pinkish relics are glacial erratics, transported here from the distant outcrops at Shap in the Lake District by an ice sheet some 13,000 years ago.

Beyond a second stile, walk ahead a few paces before turning left along a broad field-edge track that borders woodland. At the first wall turn right and – wall on your left – walk ahead towards the ruined farm at West Thorpe. Swap sides of the wall here and continue in the same direction to reach and use a metal field gate at a field track; from here drop half-left, aiming to pass just right of the offset field corner and then right of the cattle-byre to a stone stile into a lane at the southern end of Whorlton Bridge. Cross the bridge – a remarkable cast-iron, chain suspension bridge with wooden decking, built in 1831 – and take the fingerposted flight of steps that rises steeply behind the old toll house at the far end **E**.

At the top, the main route of this walk forks left along the path beside the garden wall. A short diversion ahead on the road reveals **Fernaville's Rest Inn** at the far end of the substantial village green here in pretty Whorlton, just 400 yds distant. Back on the main walk, use the hand-gate beyond the cottages and walk along the left edge of a string of fields linked by hand-gates. Beyond the third gate drop through a strip of woodland and, at the far side, keep ahead as the path bends sharp right, go through the waymarked field gate and trace a path along the top of a slope dappled by fine old oaks. Drop gradually left to the first of another

Meeting of the Waters

string of hand-gates outside the woodland edge, presently reaching a stile into these woods. Walk within the top of the woods on a narrow path, drop to cross a footbridge over Sledwich Gill and climb the stone stile at the far side to continue along the left edge of fields high above the Tees .

A final woodside hand-gate **F** occurs where the trees drop away to the left. Use this gate and walk ahead beside the stone wall at the head of the steeply sloping pasture (*Meeting of the Waters* is down to your left here). Pass through another hand-gate at the far end and walk to the immediate left of the lone ash tree; from the spring here look ahead left for a stone step stile through the cross-wall, walk to and use this and then drop to the far left corner of the field to a stile. Trace the path outside Tees Bank Plantation; about 150 yds beyond the next stile look for the waymarked gate on your left showing the way onto a woodland path. At the end of the woods the path continues along the foot of fields, presently meeting a road at the far end of a sloping pasture below a farm complex. Turn back-left, cross Abbey Bridge and turn right along Abbey Road before forking left to return to the car park. ●

Cauldron Snout

		GPS waypoints
Start	Reservoir Viewpoint, Cow Green Reservoir, 10 miles (16km) north-west of Middleton-in-Teesdale	✎ NY 810 309 Ⓐ NY 847 309
Distance	7¼ miles (11.7km)	Ⓑ NY 837 296
Height gain	560ft (170m)	Ⓒ NY 830 284
Approximate time	3½ hours	Ⓓ NY 814 285 Ⓔ NY 815 306
Parking	Cow Green Reservoir	
Ordnance Survey maps	Landrangers 91 (Appleby-in-Westmorland) and 92 (Barnard Castle), Explorer OL31 (North Pennines – Teesdale & Weardale)	

This is an easily accessible walk into the Moor House and Upper Teesdale National Nature Reserve – the largest in England – culminating in the memorable Cauldron Snout waterfall cascade. Most of the route is straightforward underfoot, but reaching these remote, austere acres amidst England's last great wilderness means that sections of the route are challenging, particularly below Falcon Clints and beside Cauldron Snout. In these areas the dolerite rock will be very slippery in wet weather and great care is needed. The scramble up the Whin Sill beside Cauldron Snout is not for the faint hearted or sufferers from vertigo. We strongly recommend that you wear ankle-supporting boots on this walk.

Cow Green Reservoir was filled in 1971 to supply the industrial belt of distant Teesside and Middlesbrough. Its creation caused an outcry, as the land it drowned is regarded as part of the last great vestige of immediate post-glacial landscape in England. The area remains a haven for ground-nesting birds and is also scarred by countless old rakes and shafts resulting from the mining of galena (lead ore) and barytes over many centuries. For these reasons, it is important to keep to the described route and not take advantage of the Open Access lands hereabouts. Spend a few minutes studying the interpretive boards at the car park before commencing the walk.

✎ Walk back along the reservoir access road for 1½ miles (2.4km). Keep right at the fork beyond a cattle-grid and remain on the tarred lane to reach an isolated barn and stock-pens adjoining a beck, bridge and cattle-grid Ⓐ. Cross the grid and then turn right along the gated track, a gravelled road to the Natural England offices. The track meanders through upland pastures and hay meadows rich with Teesdale's renowned wildflowers from May to July. Approaching Widdy Bank Farm, the great wall of the Whin Sill – here called Cronkley Scar – dominates the view, a harbinger of things to come.

Pass through the yard in front of the farm, join the Pennine Way and follow

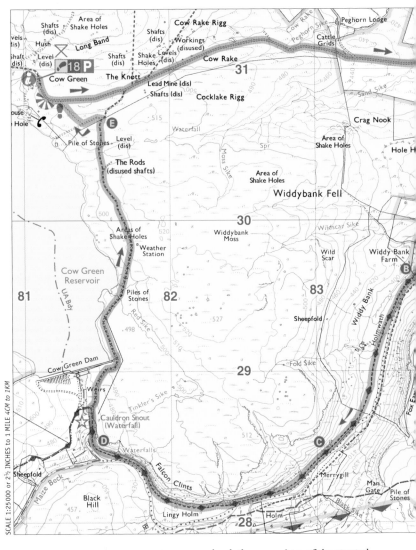

SCALE 1:25 000 or 2½ INCHES to 1 MILE 4CM to 1KM

the roughening track beside the river
B. This is a marvellous section of the
route, with the boulder-strewn Tees
coursing beneath the steep slopes and
looming crags formed from the Great
Whin Sill. This vast landscape feature
was created by molten rock rising through
and penetrating layers of limestone and
other rocks 295 million years ago,
solidifying as a resistant outcrop of rock
geologists call dolerite. On the opposite
bank there are signs of the stunted
juniper trees for which this area is
internationally important; at one point an
island in the river is covered by these.

Beyond a kissing-gate **C** the track
soon narrows to a strip between craggy
slopes and the Tees; shortly it crosses
the first of a long series of boulder
fields – *take care here, particularly in
wet weather when the rocks are very
slippery*. The path picks a way below
the cliffs of Falcon Clints to reach a
point where the Tees is joined by Maize
Beck, a confluence overlooked by a

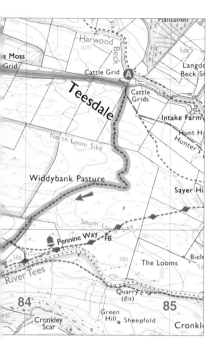

cataract. The distinctive columnar joints of the dolerite rock are particularly noticeable in this area (the famous Giant's Causeway is the best-known example). Here, the path is a sliver up these, immediately beside the falls – *proceed with patience and care when tackling this four-limb scramble.* Beyond the top of the falls, turn right along the service road. Follow it past the dam and across the moorland above the eastern bank of Cow Green Reservoir. Along the way, just before the weather station, there is an outcrop of unusual sugar limestone, a kind of marble created by the heat of those volcanic intrusions of aeons ago. Rare plants occur here, including Spring Gentian, unique to this site in mainland Britain. Farther on, distinctive rakes scar the surface and capped shafts mark the site of Rodd's Vein, an old barytes mine.

Go through the gate **E** marking the boundary of the Nature Reserve and turn left on the rough track. In 150 yds fork right on a path that ends up on the road near the car park. ●

solid stone byre. Turn right and the thundering sound of tumbling water bounces off the gorge sides.

Cauldron Snout **D** has formed where the Tees has chiselled a way down through the Whin Sill over a spectacular

Cauldron Snout

Talkin Tarn and Gelt Woods

Talkin Tarn and Gelt Woods

		GPS waypoints
Start	Talkin Tarn Country Park, south of Brampton	🥾 NY 543 591
Distance	6 miles (9.7km)	Ⓐ NY 544 596
Height gain	310ft (95m)	Ⓑ NY 531 595
Approximate time	3 hours	Ⓒ NY 527 587
Parking	Talkin Tarn Country Park (Pay and Display)	Ⓓ NY 532 573
		Ⓔ NY 541 561
Ordnance Survey maps	Landranger 86 (Haltwhistle & Brampton), Explorer 315 (Carlisle)	Ⓕ NY 549 573
		Ⓖ NY 543 583

There are three main focal points on this varied walk in the countryside just to the east of Carlisle. First comes a highly attractive and tranquil tarn that is the centrepiece of a country park. Second, there is a spectacular walk through the thickly wooded gorge of the River Gelt. Third, the route passes through the pleasant and quiet village of Talkin. The walk ends with a relaxing stroll beside Talkin Tarn. Apart from some 'up and down' walking through the gorge, with some rocky paths in places, this is an easy and well-waymarked route, with no steep ascents or difficult stretches.

🥾 Walk from the car park to the tarn and turn left to pass by the **Boathouse Tearoom**. In 130 yds turn left at a fingerpost for Brampton Junction and walk the path ahead to the far side of the woods. Here, use a kissing-gate (signed for Brampton Fell Road) and skirt the left edge of the field, shortly merging with a field side track which reaches a tarred lane Ⓐ.

Turn left along the lane for just under ¹/₂ mile (800m), crossing a railway line, and at a T-junction keep ahead along a track, at a public footpath sign to Brampton and Gelt Woods. Descend gently to go through a metal gate, keep ahead to pass beside a farm; keep ahead on the track for 200 yds and turn left, at a fingerpost Ⓑ for Gelt Woods, along

the rough drive to Unity. Just before the farm, fork right towards a barn, use the field gate above the cottage and then pass to the right side of the barn, putting a wall on your left. Walk alongside this to reach Gelt Woods.

Climb the stile Ⓒ and walk ahead 10 paces into the trees. Turn left and, at the nearby fork, left again towards Middle Gelt, commencing a beautiful walk up the sylvan gorge. The path drops beside metal railings, becomes a sunken track and then undulates beside old river cliffs and quarried faces high above the lively River Gelt. In about 500 yds, just past a particularly colourful river cliff on your left, fork left – along the wider path beneath tall pines – and shortly climb wide-spaced steps before descending

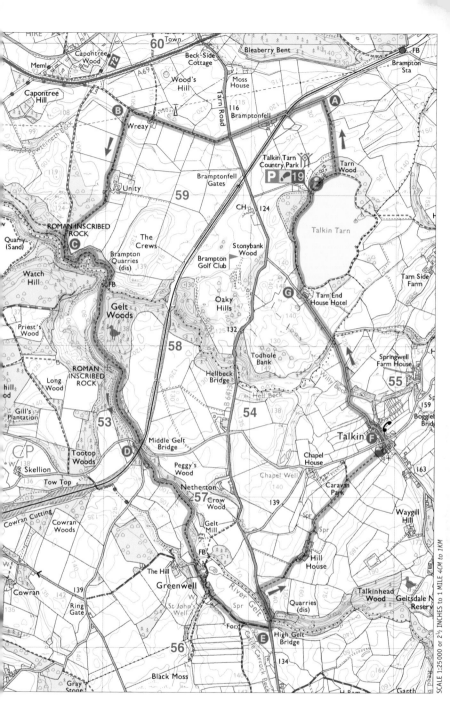

again to cross a bridge over a side-beck.
The route climbs again, leaving the
riverside before again rejoining it,
eventually reaching a lane **D** beneath a
railway viaduct.

Turn right, cross the bridge and turn

left on the lane for Greenwell. In 150 yds
take the path on the left, signed for
Greenwell. Climb a stile and pick up a

A corner of Talkin Tarn

riverside path, following this south via redundant and current stiles to a stile onto a partly boardwalked fence-side path beside rough pasture, ending at a step-stile into a tarred lane. Bear left to walk through the remote hamlet of Greenwell. Go through the metal gate across the track and ahead across the gravelled yard in front of cottages. Use a further gate at the far side and rise up the grassy path to join a stony lane leading away from the last house in the hamlet, which leads to a main road **E**.

Turn left, cross High Gelt Bridge and carefully walk this winding road to reach the far end of the woods on your right. Here, take the stile signed for Talkin and drift left up the field to join the line of a wall on your left. At the far end of this, turn left along the walled track, shortly bearing right up a tarred lane to reach Hill House Farm. The way through the farmyard is well waymarked

– the way out is along a track between slurry and silage units. Beyond the complex, go through a gate and keep along the left edge of two fields. From the gate leaving this last field, walk ahead right, aiming to meet the far hedge line about 50 yds below the imposing stone house and chapel. Use the hand-gate, cross the horse pasture and use a stile beside a gate. Walk ahead-left, across the driveway and towards the white-painted buildings, where stone steps drop into the car park of The **Blacksmiths Arms** pub. Turn left to reach the village centre crossroads in Talkin **F**.

Keep ahead, towards Talkin Tarn and Brampton, tracing this quiet lane for $^3/_4$ mile (1.2km) to reach a complex of buildings. Just past these, use the kissing-gate **G** on your right and walk through to join the path beside Talkin Tarn. Turn left and follow this back to the Boathouse Tearoom. ●

Wolsingham and the Weardale Way

		GPS waypoints
Start	Wolsingham, Weardale	✐ NZ 073 366
Distance	7½ miles (12km)	Ⓐ NZ 072 356
Height gain	785ft (240m)	Ⓑ NZ 063 349
Approximate time	3 hours	Ⓒ NZ 042 344
Parking	Lay-by on the Hamsterley Road at Wear Bank, south of Wolsingham Bridge opposite the driveway to Ashes House	Ⓓ NZ 038 364
		Ⓔ NZ 047 367
Ordnance Survey maps	Landranger 92 (Barnard Castle), Explorer OL31 (North Pennines – Teesdale & Weardale)	

The middle Wear Valley is an exceptionally pretty area of countryside. A short climb at the start of this walk is rewarded with far-reaching views across miles of heather-burnished hills and an airy walk beside an archetypical Pennine grouse moor, whilst the river's tussles with the limestone, offer a relaxing finale of riverside walking on the Weardale Way. Wolsingham is an enticing little town, with charming buildings and a heritage railway to explore.

✐ Look for the ladder-stile at the bottom end of the lay-by, just below the field gate. Climb this and turn right up the steep pasture. Climb the stile at the left end of a short section of walling and drift slightly left to use a stile into the corner of a field just above a tree stump and over a track. Walk up the left edge of this field, slip through the gate in the top left corner and turn right alongside a wall. Pass through two gates and walk to the right of the barn to reach a driveway near Chatterley Farm. Turn right along this. At the end, turn left up the road; at the sharp left bend keep ahead up the 'No Through Road' and bend right to reach a hairpin left bend Ⓐ.

Fork right along the rougher lane here, rising imperceptibly along the edge of the huge tract of moorland that stretches across Pikeston Fell to the hidden Hamsterley Forest, secluded in deep valleys several miles to the south. Simply remain with this moorland-edge way, enjoying the ever-unfolding views into upper Weardale and encompassing the distant, dark wall of the Cleveland Hills way to the south. As the lane bends left to a secluded house set in trees, keep ahead through the gate Ⓑ and remain on the keeper's road, a stand of pines on your right. Far ahead on the skyline is a clump of trees known locally as the Elephant Trees; these are your next target.

One field before them, go through the gate on the right Ⓒ and walk down the sloping field, gradually drifting away from the wall on your right.

Almost immediately a circular

sheepfold with fir trees growing within its walls comes into view below. Pass to the right of this, continuing to follow the wall on your right. Having gone through the gate at the bottom of this field, you pass another circular sheepfold, this time on your right. The path joins a track that curves round the hill to a gate in the lower, left-hand corner of the field. Go through this gate; the flooded Frosterley quarries are in sight below as the track bends to the right just before the bottom left field corner and becomes more pronounced. Before the next walled corner go through the gate, left, to reach West Biggins Farm. Pass in front of the farmhouse and then allow the track to curve right past a small pond, whilst you use gates between the barns and sheep-pens, bending left along the farm's access road as it drops gently towards the Wear.

At the junction above the former Hope Quarry **D**, fork right through a gateway and continue along the dirt road, shortly passing left of a barn. Remain on this tree-shaded track which, beyond a gate, skirts the bottom edge of fields before bending right to enter the yard at Landieu Farm. Go through the farmyard and bend left along the access road, soon reaching a crossing of the Weardale Railway **E**. Cross carefully and then turn right along the tarred road that leaves the caravan park at this point. The manicured greensward contrasts with the swirling river just to your left; at this point you've joined the Weardale Way, on which you remain for the rest of the walk.

When the drive bears off to the left to cross the bridge over the Wear, keep straight on along a narrow footpath with the river close to the left. The sound of rushing water heralds a weir, opposite which the path goes through a small gate, across a footbridge and into a long, narrow meadow. Keep to the

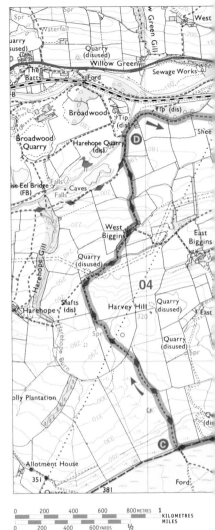

right-hand side of this, close to the railway. The walking is pleasant here on sheep-cropped turf as it is through a second, even longer meadow.

The river is now some distance to the left. Go over another footbridge into a third narrow meadow, still keeping to the railway side – but do not head for the tempting white gate at the end.

Soon you can see the road bridge over the railway ahead; go up the steps to the road and turn right. The brief climb that follows to return to the starting place is the most taxing that is encountered on this route. ●

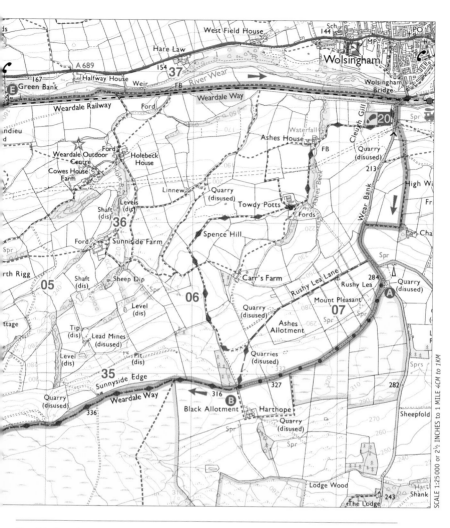

SCALE 1:25 000 or 2½ INCHES to 1 MILE 4CM to 1KM

Weardale from The Elephant Trees

Alston and the South Tyne Valley

Start	Alston Station
Distance	6¼ miles (10km)
Height gain	475ft (145m)
Approximate time	3 hours
Parking	Alston Station
Ordnance Survey maps	Landranger 86 (Haltwhistle & Brampton), Explorer OL31 (North Pennines – Teesdale & Weardale)

GPS waypoints

- 🥾 NY 716 467
- Ⓐ NY 715 461
- Ⓑ NY 708 474
- Ⓒ NY 702 473
- Ⓓ NY 698 478
- Ⓔ NY 695 490
- Ⓕ NY 695 496

After leaving Alston, the first part of the walk follows the Pennine Way – sometimes across rough, grassy moorland – past the striking Roman fort of Epiacum and on to Kirkhaugh. The return leg is along the South Tyne Trail, a footpath that keeps beside the track of the South Tynedale Railway back to Alston Station. On both legs of the route there are fine views over the valley of the South Tyne to the enveloping stark moorlands.

The former lead-mining town of Alston is situated in the upper reaches of the South Tyne valley and claims to be the highest market town in England. It retains a pleasantly unchanged and 'off the beaten track' air, with steep, cobbled streets and narrow alleys radiating from the Market Square. The imposing Victorian church was built in 1869.

The station served a branch line, opened in 1852 to link Alston with the main Carlisle–Newcastle line at Haltwhistle. It closed in 1976, and since 1983 part of its length has been operated by the narrow-gauge South Tynedale Railway, using a mixture of steam and diesel locomotives.

🥾 Begin by walking up to the road and turn right through Alston. Just after bending right to cross the bridge over the South Tyne, turn right by a war memorial and almost immediately right

again Ⓐ along a track through trees, at a Pennine Way sign. Keep left, pass through the parking area and join a track that leads to an isolated house. Use the hand gate and walk the enclosed path left of the grounds, climb a stile and walk along the right-hand edge of several pastures to reach a field-gate and hand-gate between ornate gateposts. Pass through and bear left, rising to a waymarked path that passes to the left of the smaller house here.

Go through a gate immediately beyond and turn right, skirt the field edge round to a fingerpost and a stone stile into a rough lane; turn left up this to the main road. Turn right to find, on the left in 150 yds, a Pennine Way fingerpost for Slaggyford Ⓑ.

Use the hand-gate; then another gate to the right of the barn. A steepening grassy path now rises beside the wall on

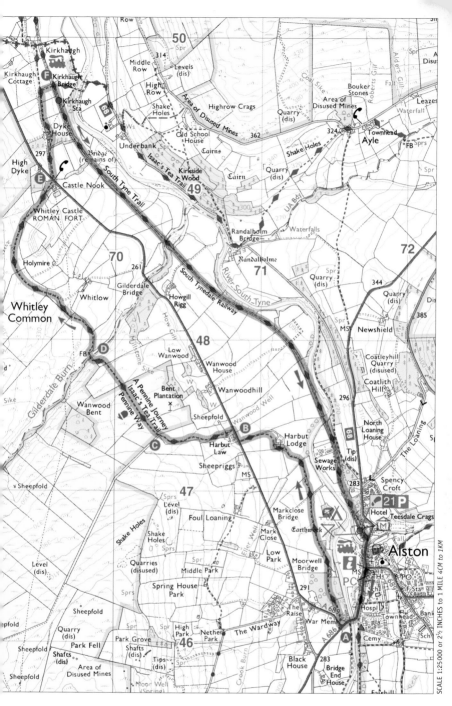

your left; follow this past the offset corner and gradually drift right to find a stile in the top right corner **C**.

Once over this, keep ahead across fields, heading just left of the distant farm and using hand gates through two walls. Excellent, all-round views sweep across Whitley Common to the high moors and fells and east towards the

Gilderdale Burn

heart of the old lead-mining country. After a stile, the path drops down into the sharp valley of Gilderdale Burn.

Cross the footbridge here **D**, climb the stile at the end and bear right up the narrow path, a wall on your right. Beyond a boggy section, the path veers slightly left to a ladder-stile, once over which bear right, joining a rough field road. In around 50 yds, turn left off this track and walk up the pitted field, parallel to a fence off to your left. You'll soon find another field road; bear left along this to reach a ladder-stile to the right of the right-hand of two gates.

Climb the stile, keep ahead to go through a metal gate and continue along the track, which curves right, keeping parallel to a wall on the right. Beyond the wall are the striking earthworks of the Roman fort of Epiacum, built to guard one of the main routes to Hadrian's Wall. The track heads downhill to join the wall, where you turn right over a ladder-stile. Bear left, head downhill towards farm buildings, above a small burn on the left, and climb a stile. Continue down a narrow path, which bends sharply left to cross

a footbridge over the burn and then winds down through trees to climb a stone stile onto a road **E**.

Cross over, go through the gate and turn left across the top of the pasture, walking to pass the top of the line of tall pines. Beyond a gate, a stile over a wood-rail fence takes the path to the right of the house and grounds here, past which look for the waymarked gate in the far top corner of the sloping field. Go through another gate and keep along the top of the field to a third gate. The Pennine Way goes ahead here, but you now turn right, down the left edge of the field to a bridge over the South Tynedale Railway **G**.

Cross the bridge, turn right and drop to the nearby stile on your right. Climb this and turn left, passing Kirkhaugh Station on a path beside the railway which you now follow all the way back to Alston. High bridges, wildflowers and some good views of the River South Tyne all add interest; towards the end, the path passes by the railway's workshops and changes sides of the main line here. Shortly thereafter, the path reaches the station car park in Alston. ●

Waskerley Way

		GPS waypoints
Start	Waskerley, 6 miles (9.7km) south-west of Consett	✎ NZ 050 453
Distance	7½ miles (12.1km). Shorter version 5½ miles (8.9km)	Ⓐ NZ 058 451
		Ⓑ NZ 077 478
Height gain	705ft (215m). Shorter version 475ft (145m)	Ⓒ NZ 077 484
		Ⓓ NZ 064 485
Approximate time	4 hours (3 hours for the shorter version)	Ⓔ NZ 054 487
		Ⓕ NZ 056 484
Parking	Waskerley Picnic Site	Ⓖ NZ 059 471
		Ⓗ NZ 058 462
Ordnance Survey maps	Landrangers 87 (Hexham & Haltwhistle) and 88 (Newcastle upon Tyne), Explorer 307 (Consett & Derwent Reservoir)	

The trackbeds of disused railways provide many excellent walks in County Durham: this route uses a section of one of the oldest of these. Originally built in 1834 to transport limestone and iron ore from Weardale to Consett, it was later owned by that most famous of railway companies, the Stockton & Darlington. The return from Castleside passes through a variety of terrain. Much of it is on field paths, but quiet lanes, moorland and woodland tracks are used as well. A shorter version is also offered.

It seems incredible today that the lofty, remote moorland hamlet of Waskerley was once a busy railway centre, having a locomotive shed that housed six engines. Only a few buildings survive from its heyday, amongst them the chapel. The line was closed in 1968.

✎ Leave the picnic site and turn left along the old railway track, passing what could have been the engine shed, with heavily buttressed walls, and the chapel. There is a wide view beyond; the Cheviots can be seen on a clear day. Waskerley stands at 1,150ft (350m) above sea-level. There is a planting of conifers in the broad cutting where once there were sidings. Pass a seat Ⓐ thoughtfully sited at an excellent viewpoint and a little farther on go through the gate on the left onto the

track to Red House, thus cutting off a corner. The Waskerley Way officially goes on to Burnhill Junction, where it joined a later railway going to Crook and Darlington; if you take this longer route you would turn sharply left to reach Red House.

Turn left at Red House onto the Waskerley Way again. On a windy day it may be wise to walk at the bottom of the deep cutting but then you miss the view that you can enjoy from the path along the top. Over to the left is Nanny Mayer's Incline, where full trucks loaded with ore or limestone were used to haul empty ones back up to Waskerley. Mrs Mayer kept a pub close by.

The deep cutting is followed by a broad, high embankment fringed with rowans. After a bridge the old course of

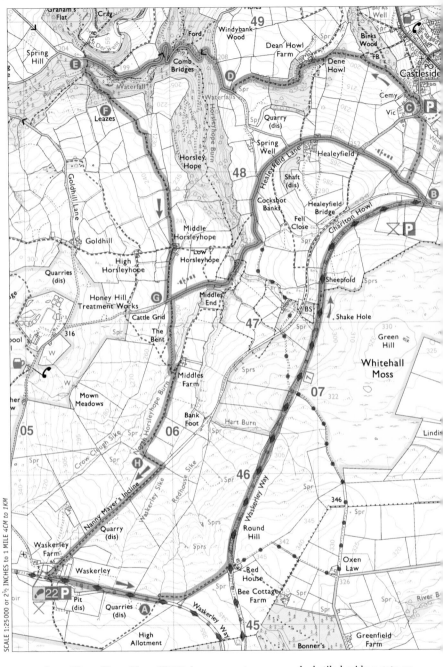

the line from the incline joins from the left. A little distance after, you will come to the White Hall picnic place **B** where the Waskerley Way meets a road. Turn left and walk this road for 300 yds to a waymarked stile beside a gate on your right. *(The shorter option of this walk entails remaining on this road [Healeyfield Lane], keep left at the junction and rejoin the full walk at Point **G**.)*

For the full route, climb the stile and walk along the field road beyond; as this fades at the corner of fencing, head slightly right to a gate through a wire cross-fence and then walk half left, downhill to the large patch of gorse in the bottom left corner. A stile here leads into a picnic area and car park **C**.

Turn right up the road for 50 paces before forking left along a footpath waymarked at an old cobbled entry, leading to a lovely wooded valley. After this, pass through the gate and walk along the edge of the field with a fence on the right. A track leads on past Dene Howl Farm on the right and then climbs a narrow, steep-sided and dry valley. This resembles Devon more than Durham.

Turn right at the road **D** and descend a steep hill, twisting down to Comb Bridges; look for footpaths to cut off hairpin bends.

Climb the lane on the other side of the bridge. Soon a ridge is reached – a narrow neck of land with woods dropping away on both sides, separating the valley of the River Derwent from that of the Hisehope Burn. The lane levels out and passes by two fields on your right. Some 300 yds after re-entering

woodland, look for a waymarked stile on the left **E**. A path drops steeply down through the woods to cross a footbridge over the burn. Turn left off the bridge along a narrow path that shortly widens and starts to climb the steep, wooded slope, presently reaching a fence within the woods. Keep this on your right and walk up the path to emerge via a hand-gate into a field corner **F**.

Head a shade left over the brow of the field to find and use a gate in a short section of stone walling. Stay close to the left edge of a series of fields, which direction brings you to Middle Horsleyhope Farm. Go through the farmyard to join the drive and continue to a road **G**. *(The shorter route rejoins here – turn left if you've followed this option.)* Cross into the farm road virtually opposite and follow this through to a point just beyond a bridge over a burn (the map shows the right of way as deviating slightly off this road, but is not obvious on the ground). Once over this bridge, the road hairpins to the left; at this point, walk ahead left off the bend, rising up the bank to a line of wall at some pine trees.

Turn right on the rough track alongside the wall. Keep ahead beyond the last stand of pines on a thin path beside the ruinous wall-cum-fence. In a further 350 yds, **H** look left for the remains of a small building; walk to and past this to meet the obvious line of Nanny Mayer's Incline. Turn right up this and trace it up to the old chapel near the engine sheds at Waskerley. Use gates here to gain the Waskerley Way and turn right back to the car park. ●

Nanny Mayer's Incline

Appleby, Rutter Force and the River Eden

		GPS waypoints
Start	Appleby-in-Westmorland	
Distance	8½ miles (13.7km)	NY 683 204
Height gain	490ft (150m)	Ⓐ NY 683 198
Approximate time	4½ hours	Ⓑ NY 671 188
Parking	Appleby (disc or Pay and Display)	Ⓒ NY 675 175
Ordnance Survey maps	Landranger 91 (Appleby-in-Westmorland), Explorer OL19 (Howgill Fells & Upper Eden Valley)	Ⓓ NY 682 158
		Ⓔ NY 689 162
		Ⓕ NY 701 172
		Ⓖ NY 696 173
		Ⓗ NY 688 194

Take your time over this walk for there is plenty of interest and variety and much fine scenery to enjoy. It starts in an attractive riverside town, complete with medieval church and castle, and passes by an impressive waterfall to a quiet and remote village with an old church overlooking the River Eden. Finally comes a delightful ramble mostly along the edge of tree-lined meadows beside the lovely River Eden.

Appleby was the county town of Westmorland and 'in-Westmorland' was added to it as a way of perpetuating the name of the county after the local government changes of 1974 abolished it. The town lies within a horseshoe bend of the River Eden and has a fine, wide main street – Boroughgate – that slopes up from the medieval church at the bottom to the Norman castle at the top, lined by verges and old cottages. Leading off from Boroughgate is the Hospital of St Anne, an attractive courtyard of almshouses founded in 1651 by Lady Anne Clifford, who also restored the nearby castle.

🖊 Start at the bottom of Boroughgate and, with your back to the church, walk up it towards the castle and turn right in front of the castle gates. The road curves left and heads downhill. Turn right along the road

signed for Colby, bear right from the green and look on the left immediately past the white house for a footpath fingerpost for Bandley Bridge Ⓐ.

Turn along the tarmac drive, climb a stile and hug the left edge of the field to a stile into a track. Turn right; within 40 paces take the low ladder-stile on the left and walk the left side of the field to another ladder-stile into a rough lane. Turn right and walk to the end at three gates. Use the stile on the left and walk along the right-hand edge of the field. About halfway along, use the stile on your right by a boulder and head half left to another stile through a wire fence. Beyond this, keep in the same direction to crest the field; then walk to the far bottom corner and the footbridge, reached via a nearby hand-gate through a wall.

Cross Bandley Bridge Ⓑ and turn left

to use a kissing-gate in the upper field corner. Cross a stretch of boardwalk and then fork left at the waymarked junction, climb the nearby stile and turn left with a wire fence on your right. Drop down steps to join a path beside Hoff Beck and walk upstream, using a series of

stiles and following the well-walked path to reach the edge of a riverside farm complex. Use the waymarked gate into the farmyard; in 10 paces turn left through another farmyard gate and walk the walled track past the farmhouse and barns to reach the road ⒸÀ beside the walker-friendly **New Inn** at Hoff.

Cross into the lane for Oakbeck and Drybeck and follow this for 350 yds. Just past two huge ash trees, turn left along the gated track at a fingerpost for Rutter Force. Shortly after a second gate fork left to use a footbridge over Hoff Beck and then turn right, following it upstream over a string of stiles. Ignore the farm bridge, remaining on the left bank to find and cross a footbridge; then continue upstream on the right bank, the path eventually reaches a lane just above Rutter Mill, cottages and the powerful Rutter Force waterfall.

Cross the footbridge Ⓓ – this is where you get the best view of the fall – and walk along a lane up to a T-junction. Turn left and at a public footpath sign to Ormside, turn right over a stile and head gently uphill along the right-hand field edge. After climbing a stile on the brow, a grand view unfolds ahead of the impressive peaks of the North Pennines. Keep ahead over another stile and bear left across the next field to climb a stile onto a lane in front of a cottage Ⓔ. Turn left and follow the switchback lane – over a crossroads and under a railway bridge – into the small village of Great Ormside.

Continue through the village to the hall, originally a 14th-century peel tower, and the church at the far end. The sturdy Norman church with a low saddleback tower, almost fortress-like, occupies a fine position overlooking the Eden and Ormside Viaduct. The site is an ancient one, possibly a Viking burial ground.

Walk back through the village to the stile beside a post box on your right Ⓕ, signed as a footpath to Appleby. Walk the fenced path to another stile, pass

Rutter Force

left of the pond and walk across the waist of this sloping field on a level path to a gate into a rough lane. Turn left and walk to and beneath the railway bridge. Climb the ladder-stile ahead here, walk the left field edge and bend left into a wide green track, following this down to reach a gatepost and a stile on your right Ⓖ.

Use the stile and follow the sunken track along the right-hand field edge to climb a stile into the woods. Drop to use a footbridge and then climb steeply beside a fence on your right. Slip over a stile and turn left on a path within the woodland's top edge. This meanders high above the River Eden for about 600 yds before bending right at a waymarked post; then falls down a long flight of steps to become a riverside path, heading downstream beside the Eden. The path eventually leaves the woodland and traces a riverside fence beside several meadows.

At the narrow neck of a field use the stile Ⓗ at the left corner to join a narrow path running along the foot of woods on your left. This emerges via a kissing-gate into a lane; turn left to the main road and here bear right, keeping right to reach the memorial at the top of Boroughgate outside the castle gates. Walk downhill into Appleby town centre. ●

Barnard Castle, Cotherstone and the River Tees

		GPS waypoints
Start	Barnard Castle	🖊 NZ 050 163
Distance	8½ miles (13.7km)	Ⓐ NZ 045 167
Height gain	575ft (175m)	Ⓑ NZ 038 175
Approximate time	4 hours	Ⓒ NZ 023 191
Parking	Barnard Castle (Pay and Display)	Ⓓ NZ 013 193
Ordnance Survey maps	Landranger 92 (Barnard Castle), Explorer OL31 (North Pennines – Teesdale & Weardale)	Ⓔ NZ 009 200
		Ⓕ NZ 013 202
		Ⓖ NZ 032 184

Almost the whole of this walk is along the well-waymarked Teesdale Way. The outward route keeps above the south bank of the river to the attractive village of Cotherstone and crosses the Tees a little farther on. The return leg is above the north side and, after descending the steep wooded banks, the last 1½ miles (2.4km) is beside the river itself, a delightful and relaxing finale. Although quite a lengthy and undulating route, there is no particularly steep or difficult climbing. With magnificent views up and down Teesdale, beautiful woodland and grand riverside walking, it is worth taking plenty of time over this outstanding and highly memorable walk.

Barnard Castle occupies a fine position above the River Tees, its main street, lined by dignified stone buildings, sloping down to the old bridge over the river. In the town centre stands the 18th-century Market Cross, once used for the selling of dairy produce, hence its alternative name of Butter Cross. Nearby is the large medieval church, founded around the same time as the castle. It retains some Norman work, especially in the nave, but was enlarged and remodelled over the succeeding centuries, particularly in the 15th century under Richard, Duke of Gloucester, later Richard III.

The town gets its name from the castle built by Bernard de Baliol in the 12th century. Its ruins, dominated by a circular tower, crown a long ridge above the Tees and look particularly impressive when seen from the river. On the east side of the town is the massive Bowes Museum, built in the 19th century in the style of a French château by John and Josephine Bowes. It is well worth a visit and houses a fine collection of paintings, furniture, costume and ceramics.

🖊 From the Market Cross building walk along the main street, the Raby Arms on your right. Upon reaching the sharp bend at the foot of Galgate, turn left beside the Methodist Church and walk along the tarred driveway to the fork. The castle entrance is to the left of

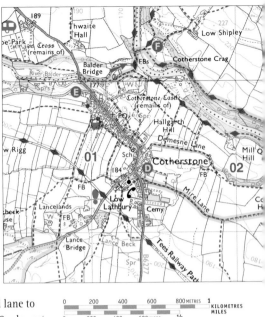

the green; our route is straight ahead and down the rougher, winding track to the right that twists down to a riverside path and the near end of a bridge across the River Tees **A**.

This is Deepdale Aqueduct, built in 1893 to carry water from the reservoirs in Baldersdale. Walk across this (a classic view of Barnard Castle is downstream); turn right along the road at the end and first right along a tarred driveway. Climb the stile and remain on this tarred lane to enter Pecknell Wood; some 110 yds past the cottage, fork right onto a narrow path beneath firs and walk this to and up a flight of steps onto the old railway line at the west end of a demolished viaduct **B**.

Climb the nearby stile and walk the right edge of the field to use another stile on your right in 100 yds. Turn left (Teesdale Way disc) and trace the left edge of the pasture to a further stile in the far corner leading into a track. Turn right towards the farm, but before reaching this turn left at a waymarked junction, go through a gate and walk beside the fence on your right. At the corner turn right, remaining beside the fence before turning left outside the woodland edge. At the next corner use a hand-gate; drop to and cross a footbridge and climb up to regain the woodland edge route. Remain with the path just outside the woods, using several more hand-gates and another footbridge before reaching a point where a hand-gate offers access into the woodland. Descend the steep path beneath the fir-trees; at the foot of the woods climb a stile and bear right to use a small slab-bridge. Walk ahead to

find a field road trending up and left across the flank of a hillside, leading to a grassy terrace. Remain on this to and over a stile and walk to a gate to the right of a barn. Stick to the right of the pasture, shortly crossing a stile before walking the right-edge of a field to reach the edge of a country house's garden **C**.

Do not use the gate here; instead turn left outside the fence, climb a stone stile and walk along the rough drive away from Cooper House. Beyond a gate this becomes a hedged lane leading through to the edge of the pretty village of Cotherstone. Turn right along the road **D**, bear right at the junction and then pass to the left of the first village green. Continue, to pass to the right of the second, sloping green and downhill to a fingerpost about 100 yds before a bridge over the River Balder **E**. Use the gap-stile on the right here, descend steps and follow a well-waymarked path beside the river. The path soon bears right to continue, by a hedge on the left and below an embankment on the right, to a gate. Go through and turn

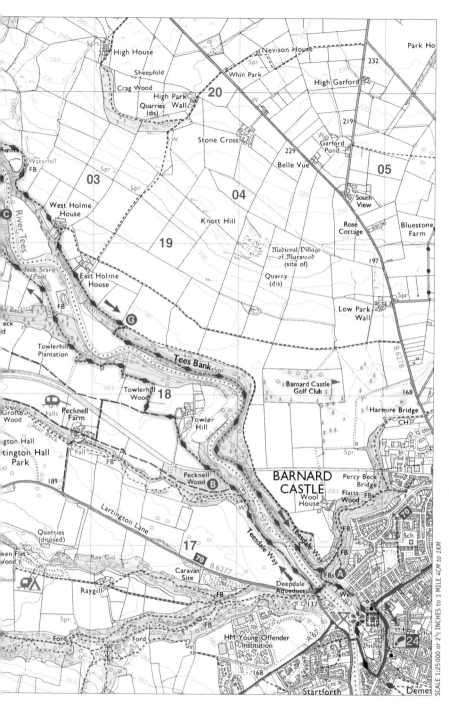

left along a tarmac track, which bears right and continues down to the River Tees. At a Teesdale Way post, turn left to cross a footbridge over the Balder – by its confluence with the Tees – continue by the Tees and turn right to cross a footbridge over it.

Turn right **F**, head across a meadow and on the far side cross footbridge over a small beck and follow a path into riverside woods. The path climbs steeply to a stile. Climb it, walk along the top

SCALE 1:25000 or 2½ INCHES to 1 MILE 4CM to 1KM

inside edge of the woodland, by a wall on the left, climb a stone stile in that wall and continue – now with the wall on the right – to a stile in the field corner. After climbing that, follow a switchback route along the right-hand edge of a field, go through a gate, continue along the right-hand edge of the next field but, where the wall bears right, keep straight ahead, making for a stone stile in the wall on the far side.

Climb it, turn right down a steep embankment to cross a footbridge over a beck and turn right onto a path above the beck, which heads up to keep by a wire fence on the left. The path bends left to continue once more along the top edge of steeply sloping riverside woods. Climb a stile, walk along a track to climb another one and continue towards a farm. After climbing the next stile, keep ahead to pass in front of the farmhouse and climb a ladder-stile. Bear right on a path outside the top of the woods, crossing a series of three stiles.

Just beyond the third stile, take the waymarked hand-gate **G** on your right and drop down the steep path through the woods to another gate into riverside pasture. Turn left, shortly re-entering the woods. From this point the path undulates beside or above the Tees – in places requiring some sure-footed work – before crossing a footbridge across Percy Beck; turn right to reach the Deepdale Aqueduct. From here, retrace your route back to the Castle Park. ●

Barnard Castle rising above the River Tees

High and Low Force

		GPS waypoints	
Start	Bowlees Visitor Centre, 3 miles (4.8km) north-west of Middleton-in-Teesdale	🖉	NY 907 282
		Ⓐ	NY 903 278
		Ⓑ	NY 881 284
Distance	8½ miles (13.7km)	Ⓒ	NY 861 282
Height gain	900ft (275m)	Ⓓ	NY 862 293
Approximate time	4½ hours	Ⓔ	NY 854 302
Parking	Bowlees Visitor Centre	Ⓕ	NY 862 305
		Ⓖ	NY 867 298
Ordnance Survey maps	Landrangers 91 (Appleby-in-Westmorland) or 92 (Barnard Castle), Explorer OL31 (North Pennines – Teesdale & Weardale)	Ⓗ	NY 890 289

The path by the River Tees upstream from Low to High Force is one of the best-known footpaths in the north. This is understandable for it not only provides the best viewpoint for one of the most spectacular British waterfalls but is also a superb riverside walk in itself. The return is on little-used paths and byways along the north side of the valley and is hardly less enjoyable. If a more taxing route is needed, this can be combined with Walk 18 to take in another famous cascade – Cauldron Snout. This would cover a distance of about 17 miles (27km).

🖉 From Bowlees car park, cross the bridge to the visitor centre, which contains an exhibition illustrating the natural and human history of the area. From here go down the short lane to reach the main road. Look right for a hand-gate and footpath sign for Low Force and join the firm path across pastures to a gap-stile into woodland. This leads to Wynch Bridge Ⓐ, a lovely suspension bridge spanning a ravine just below the cataract of Low Force. This series of falls is more beautiful than High Force and offers photographers the opportunity of a wider range of viewpoints.

Cross the bridge and turn right along the well-walked path, shortly passing a sculpture of Swaledale sheep. In summer the fenced path is bordered by drifts of colourful scabious; spend a little time beside the Tees and you'll see dippers and wagtails feeding in the boulder-strewn channels. Several stiles take you to and past the footbridge below Holwick Head House; remain on the left bank and rise up to the gateway into the Upper Teesdale National Nature Reserve. The path now threads through the distinctive woodland of stunted juniper bushes, the largest such in the country. At a small grassy clearing in the thickest part of this woodland Ⓑ fork right the few paces to gain a viewpoint over High Force, one of the most powerful and impressive waterfalls in England with a main fall of 70ft (24m). *Exercise care at this viewpoint – the rocks will be slippery in wet weather.*

Return to the main path and turn right to continue upstream beside the river, shortly leaving the juniper forest behind. The working quarry on the far bank announces blasting operations by way of blasts on a hooter. On your bank a short trip left beyond a bridge reveals the delightful Bleabeck Force falls. Remain with the Pennine Way across two solid footbridges before the path curves away from the river via steps and boardwalk to climb Bracken Rigg – views back down the Tees are excellent here.

The path crests at a point marked by two milestone-style waymarkers **C**. A path to the west slips off towards Cronkley Fell and Cauldron Snout, but our route is to the right, down the slabbed Pennine Way and up alongside a wall, presently going through a hand-gate and following the marshy path down to a stile and gate below Cronkley Farm. Skirt to the left of the barn as signed, reaching the farm access road just beyond it; following this to the bridge over the Tees **D**. Cross this and turn immediately left along an often narrow path close to the water; the views to Cronkley Scar across the confluence of the Tees with Langdon Beck can be stirring or sombre, depending on the light.

At Saur Hill Bridge **E** leave the Pennine Way as it crosses the bridge; our route is to the right and along the

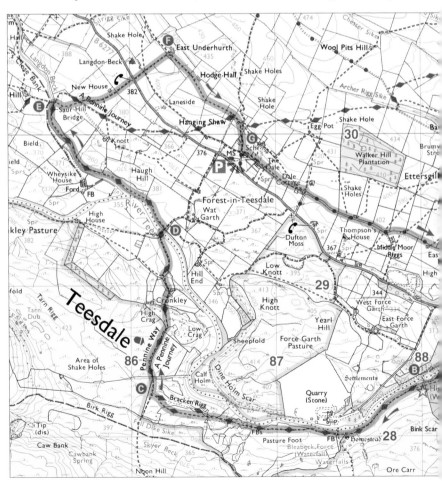

farm lane, signed for the Youth Hostel. Keep left at the junction, cross the cattle-grid and walk through to the road near to England's highest Youth Hostel at Langdon Beck. Go straight across and up the track to East Underhurth Farm. Go through the gate below the farm and, as the drive turns sharp left, go through the gate on the right **F** and walk to the abandoned Hodge Hall cottage. Fork right in front of it to find a ladder-stile in the right-hand corner. Walk slightly left across the sloping field to a field gate and track leading to the houses and barns at Hanging Shaw. Join the tarred drive here and pass through two gates to reach the tiny Forest-in-Teesdale Junior School on your left **G**.

Turn left along the lane behind the school and walk to its end, continuing beyond on an overgrown path and then along the foot of fields; pass behind Dale Cottage and rejoin a tarred lane, keeping ahead left along this. Beyond a re-purposed old chapel, this lane bends right to a farm; here, continue ahead left, go through a gate and walk beside the wall on your right. Remain on this

old track past the abandoned East Moor Riggs Farm, go through a gate and about halfway along this next field turn left down a curving field track that drops down to a gateway beside the cottage. From here walk down to the nearby tarred lane and turn right.

After ¹⁄₂ mile (800m) fork left at a junction near the end of an avenue of trees **H** to pass through the settlement of Dirt Pitt – a misnomer for a charming spot with its stream, waterfall and picturesque cottage. The name is actually a corruption of Deer Peth, a reference to an ancient hunting forest. Beyond here the lane becomes a track, dipping down to another stream. This is glorious countryside, with views through 360°. Ash Hill is passed on the right, and the woods surrounding Bowlees come into view. The final part of the walk is through delightful meadow-land (please remember to shut the gates), dipping down to reach the visitor centre, which was the starting point. ●

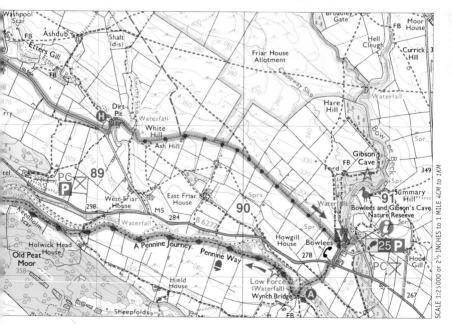

SCALE 1:25 000 or 2½ INCHES to 1 MILE 4CM to 1KM

High Cup Nick

Start	Dufton, 3 miles (4.8km) north of Appleby-in-Westmorland
Distance	8 miles (12.9km)
Height gain	1,445ft (440m)
Approximate time	4 hours
Parking	Dufton
Ordnance Survey maps	Landranger 91 (Appleby-in-Westmorland), Explorer OL19 (Howgill Fells & Upper Eden Valley)

GPS waypoints

- ✎ NY 689 249
- Ⓐ NY 693 248
- Ⓑ NY 722 250
- Ⓒ NY 745 262

The deep, narrow, perfectly U-shaped and almost geometrical chasm of High Cup Gill is one of the great natural wonders of the Pennines. This 'there and back' walk takes you along the Pennine Way to High Cup Nick at the head of the chasm. On the descent back to Dufton, there are superb views ahead all the while across the Eden valley to the Lakeland fells on the horizon. The climb is a steady and unremitting one, with no steep or strenuous sections, along generally clear and well-defined tracks. There are precipitous drops along the higher sections of the walk and the Helm wind blowing through the gap at High Cup Nick can be very strong, even on a seemingly still summer's day.

For details of Dufton, see Walk 12.

✎ Turn right out of the car park, follow the road around left- and right-hand bends out of the village and, after crossing a bridge over a beck, turn left onto a tarmac track, at a Pennine Way sign to High Cup Nick Ⓐ. Now begins a lengthy but easy and gradual climb.

The track heads gently uphill in a straight line to a gate. Go through and bear right to continue uphill along a broad, walled and rough track. Keep along the left-hand, upper track at a fork and go through two more gates. At

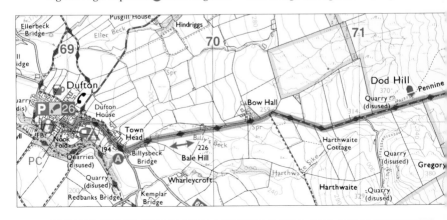

a third gate **B**, use the bridle-gate on
your left and then head slightly right up
the obvious shallow gulch, a lime-kiln
up to your left. Fork left at the first
cairn and rise to another, beyond which
a well-walked path, marked by cairns,
continues through the rocky landscape.
Later the path keeps along the rim of
High Cup Gill and there are grand
views ahead looking towards the
head of the chasm, with the bare
moorlands beyond.

At a fork, take the left-hand, upper
path – there is a waymarked stone here
– continuing across rocks, fording
several becks and finally walking along
a smooth, flat, grassy path to reach
High Cup Nick **C**. This is one of the
most dramatic viewpoints on the whole
of the Pennine Way, looking down the
length of the steep, narrow and almost
perfectly symmetrical U-shaped valley.

From here, retrace your steps to the
start. On the long descent there are
superb views ahead all the while,

High Cup Nick

looking across the Eden valley to the
line of the Lakeland fells on the
horizon, with the conically shaped
Dufton Pike nearer at hand and the
village nestling below.

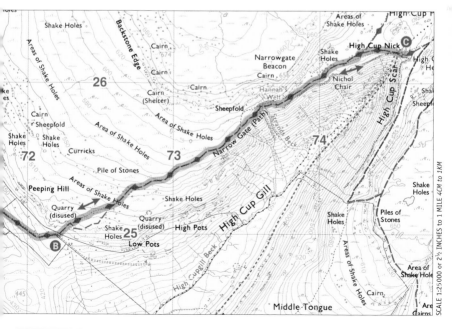

Crossthwaite Common, Rake Gill and Holwick

		GPS waypoints
Start	Middleton-in-Teesdale	
Distance	9½ miles (15.3km)	✐ NY 947 254
Height gain	1,375ft (420m)	Ⓐ NY 945 248
		Ⓑ NY 941 242
Approximate time	5 hours	Ⓒ NY 924 232
Parking	Middleton-in-Teesdale, Hill Terrace	Ⓓ NY 922 228
		Ⓔ NY 914 229
Ordnance Survey maps	Landranger 92 (Barnard Castle), Explorer OL31 (North Pennines – Teesdale & Weardale)	Ⓕ NY 910 237
		Ⓖ NY 902 258
		Ⓗ NY 900 270
		Ⓙ NY 906 269

Rising easily from the former lead-mining company town of Middleton, the walk joins the Pennine Way across the flanks of Crossthwaite Common. Parting company near a remote farm, the route (occasionally only a faint bridlepath) then strikes across heathery uplands grazed by sheep and rabbits and managed as grouse moor. During the season (12 August – 10 December) shooting parties may be encountered near Point Ⓕ; these should not affect use of the right of way, but heed advice from the shoot manager and beaters on the day. *Marvellous views of Upper Teesdale are followed by the spectacular Holwick Scar and an idyllic return to Middleton through riverside hay meadows.*

✐ From the town centre, turn down Bridge Street, the B6277 for Scotch Corner and Brough. Cross the bridge, pass the livestock market and rise to the junction where the road to Holwick turns right Ⓐ. Turn along this and look immediately left for the bridleway fingerpost for Wythes Hill and Pennine Way. Join this via the gate and trace the track over an abandoned railway and up to a waymarked gate into open access land. Use this and walk up the rutted track; in 50 paces keep ahead right on a grassy path, rising easily to a stile Ⓑ beside a gate.

From here sight a course along a path that heads towards the left side of the flat-topped hill forming the horizon. Cairns confirm the way; to your left the tree-topped conical hilltop is Kirkcarrion, a Bronze Age burial ground. Use the gate at the top corner of this rough hillside pasture and walk ahead left to a further gate; turn right through this and walk to a further gate in the cross-wall beyond the byre. Climb the step-stile just left of this and bear left to the distinctive beehive-shaped cairn and post. From this point views open out across Lunesdale; bear right towards Selset Reservoir. Climb a stile beside the next gate, pass below the clump of trees and head towards a stone barn, passing right of this via two

The River Tees below Holwick

stiles to join a moorland track. Turn left to a nearby gateway **C**.

Use the gate, follow the track for 75 yds and turn right along a path, pass through the gap-stile and head towards the farm cottage. Use a corner stile; drop to use a gate and then step across Carl Beck, rising then up the walled track to a waymarked bend 50 yds before the cottage **D**. Use the gate on the right (bridleway) and turn left alongside the wall on your left. At the point this turns 90 degrees left, look ahead for a gate in the cross-wall (not the one down on your right) and work your way across the boggy hollow to reach it. Once through, veer gradually right across reedy pasture, to put a fence on your right. There's a wide gate through this **E**, marked by an Access Land board. Use the gate and join the developing grassy track which crosses Merry Gill and rises through the fringe of newly-planted (2017) woods, passing beside a ruinous stone shelter and accompanying a fence-line to its corner. Keep ahead here, now tracing the track right of the low, rounded hilltop before dropping into Rake Gill at a shooting shelter and nearby privy **F**.

Join the inclined track behind the privy and follow this around to a walled corner. Use the gate and walk the obvious track beyond, a gully and shooting butts off to your left. In 500 yds you'll reach a marshy beck. Fork right (low footpath signboard here) along the lesser path, step across the beck and pass right of the flat-topped hill; fine views of upper Teesdale opening up. Go through a red gate and trace the path along the foot of Crooks o' Green crags. As a wall appears ahead, bear right to drop alongside this, crossing Easter

Beck beside this wall and keeping the wall on your left to reach a corner **G**.

Use the bridle-gate and walk a grassy path that bisects the angle between fence (left) and wall (right). Carefully cross Rowton Beck and walk over the low rise, heading then to and through another bridle-gate and continuing on the track, marked by cairns and standing stones, to a stile and gate just beyond the stone sheepfold on your left. Pass through and turn right on a cairned path that shortly takes the route into a cleft-like valley. Walk down this, use a bridle-gate through a wire fence and pick a path down into the cross-valley of Holwick Scars.

Cross the beck **H** and look up for a wide track that runs right, shortly passing through a gate into Holwick. Follow this tarred lane ahead to a point 120 yds past the telephone box. The way is now left at the fingerpost just before a cottage **J**. (The village pub, **The Strathmore Arms**, is a farther 600 yds along the lane; open all day, closed Tuesdays.) Go through the hand-gate and walk down the field, to and over a stile beside the barn. Continue down the next long pasture, near the foot of which a boulder with white paint on marks the way ahead. Just past this look right for a gap stile, turn left to the pasture and half-right to a stile onto a riverside path.

Turn right and follow the Tees downstream, river on your left. The Pennine Way now skirts or passes through a long series of hay meadows or departs the riverbank to pass through fingers of woodland. It is well-waymarked and eventually reaches a road near Middleton livestock market. Turn left to return to the village centre.

SCALE 1:27 777 or about 2¼ INCHES to 1 MILE 3.6CM to 1KM

0	200	400	600	800 METRES	1
					KILOMETRES
					MILES
0	200	400	600 YARDS	½

Bowes Moor

		GPS waypoints
Start	Bowes, 4 miles (6.4km) west of Barnard Castle	✎ NY 995 134
Distance	10½ miles (16.9km)	Ⓐ NY 987 133
Height gain	785ft (240m)	Ⓑ NY 973 127
		Ⓒ NY 955 129
Approximate time	5½ hours	Ⓓ NY 942 160
Parking	Bowes, Village Hall	Ⓔ NY 968 163
		Ⓕ NY 968 154
Ordnance Survey maps	Landranger 92 (Barnard Castle), Explorer OL31 (North Pennines – Teesdale & Weardale)	Ⓖ NY 972 151

On many parts of this walk there are seemingly endless vistas across wild, open and often bleak moorland. After an initial opening stretch by the delightful River Greta, the route continues along the Pennine Way over Bowes Moor, a particularly valuable and extensive area of heather moorland. A magnificent scenic walk along a ridge leads to an alternative route of the Pennine Way and this is followed across the moor and finally along a lane back to the start. Parts of the route are on faint paths – on one stretch there is no visible path at all – and there is much rough moorland walking. Therefore it is not recommended in bad weather, especially in the winter or in mist, unless you are experienced in walking in this terrain in such conditions and able to navigate by using a map and compass or a gps unit.

Bowes Castle guards the eastern end of the Stainmore route across the Pennines and, like its counterpart at Brough, which guards the western end, it stands within the earthworks of a Roman fort. The massive, square 12th-century keep is one of the largest in the country. Next to it is the small, restored Norman church.

✎ From the car park turn left along the lane to reach Gilmonby Bridge over the River Greta. Nearside of the bridge, slip right along a woodland path. This reaches pasture; at the far side of which a hand-gate up-field marks the onward route along a wide woodland path. Below; the river is dressed by mill ruins and the wide waterfalls of Mill Force.

Walk the path through the woods. Beyond another hand-gate bear right up the rough field, cross a culvert and head to a fingerpost at a stile Ⓐ well above the nearer old barn.

Turn left with the waymarked Pennine Way loop, along the gated farm lane to pass Swinholme Farm. Progress with the falling field road and cross a footbridge over the Greta. Aim slightly right to a fingerposted field-top gate; then bear right on the farm road (Pennine Way). Pass Lady Myres Farm and advance to West Charity Farm Ⓑ. Pass right of all the farm buildings (Pennine Way), then turn left out of the yard to cross a footbridge over

God's Bridge

Sleightholme Beck. Use the nearby hand-gate (ignore the beck-side path) to join a compact-surfaced field path. Curl left and remain with this through nine further hand-gates, en route passing straight over a farm road beside a river bridge (leave Pennine Way here). The path generally tracks the river (keep right at the split 60 yds past a hand-gate well beyond the path zigzag) to reach God's Bridge, a natural stone platform over the River Greta, guarded by lime-kilns. Rejoin the Pennine Way, cross the Greta and head right of the bungalow on a rising track to reach the A66 embankment. Turn left below it, use the underpass and turn right to reach a roadside farmhouse **C**.

Turn left up the continuing Pennine Way, starting a gentle climb beside a wall onto Bowes Moor. As this wall turns away right, head slightly right, soon reaching some concrete stepping stones, a post with an acorn logo and the first of a long string of cairns which chart the path – occasionally faint – across the moors. It becomes increasingly obvious as it falls to a moor-keepers road and an information board about Bowes Moor and the Pennine Way. Cross the footbridge over Deepdale Beck here and walk ahead to use the nearby gate. It's now simply a matter of keeping the wall on your right, rising constantly, if gently, to and through a hand-gate at a fence corner. Continue up beside the wall to reach the ridge-crest at a point 50 paces before a stile and Pennine Way fingerpost.

Turn right through the gate **D** (marked with blue bridleway discs), here leaving the Pennine Way in favour of a clear and grassy track that roughly parallels a fence off to your left. On clear days there are marvellous views to all points of the compass from this modest ridge. Remain on this fine moorland path for nearly two miles (3km) to reach a cross-wall/fence at a gateway.

Do not go through the gate **E**; rather, turn right along a walked path down through the reedy upland pasture, keeping parallel to the fence on your left. This is an alternative route to the Pennine Way and is discernible if narrow, twisting and occasionally boggy. Step over Hazelgill Beck and keep ahead over the rise. Put your sights on the farmhouse in the valley bottom ahead-right and walk down to this, taking any of a braided set of paths across the reedy landscape to reach a footbridge across Deepdale Beck **F** below Levy Pool Farm.

Cross the bridge and use the gate on the right; then curve left with the rough road that leads away from this remote, reed-thatched old farmhouse. Cross a cattle-grid and continue to and through a second gate to reach the junction at the driveway for West Stoney Keld Farm **G**. Turn right towards the farm buildings, but immediately before reaching them take the Pennine Way

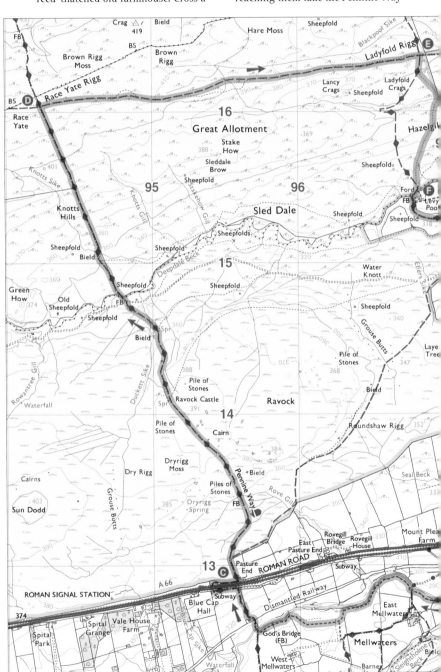

that is signposted left through a gate. Walk to the far end of the wall and turn right with it. Drop down into the clough on your left, passing well-right of the odd beehive-shaped stone structure. Your target is the barn on the hillside ahead; reach this via a gated stile over a wall.

Pass just left of the barn and climb the stone stile here, continuing ahead up the reedy field to climb a further gated stile into a lane. Turn right and walk up this; keep right at the fork just before the transmitter station and walk into Bowes village, keeping left to pass by the Ancient Unicorn inn and reach the mini-roundabout above the village hall. ●

Further Information

 ## The National Trust

Anyone who likes visiting places of natural beauty and/or historic interest has cause to be grateful to the National Trust. Without it, many such places would probably have vanished by now.

It was in response to the pressures on the countryside posed by the relentless march of Victorian industrialisation that the trust was set up in 1895. Its founders, inspired by the common goals of protecting and conserving Britain's national heritage and widening public access to it, were Sir Robert Hunter, Octavia Hill and Canon Rawnsley: respectively a solicitor, a social reformer and a clergyman. The latter was particularly influential. As a canon of Carlisle Cathedral and vicar of Crosthwaite (near Keswick), he was concerned about threats to the Lake District and had already been active in protecting footpaths and promoting public access to open countryside. After the flooding of Thirlmere in 1879 to create a large reservoir, he became increasingly convinced that the only effective way to guarantee protection was outright ownership of land.

The purpose of the National Trust is to preserve areas of natural beauty and sites of historic interest by acquisition, holding them in trust for the nation and making them available for public access and enjoyment. Some of its properties have been acquired through purchase, but many have been donated. Nowadays it is not only one of the biggest landowners in the country, but also one of the most active conservation charities, protecting 581,113 acres (253,176 ha) of land, including 555 miles (892km) of coastline, and more than 300 historic properties in England, Wales and Northern Ireland. (There is a separate National Trust for Scotland, which was set up in 1931.)

Furthermore, once a piece of land has come under National Trust ownership, it is difficult for its status to be altered. As a result of parliamentary legislation in 1907, the Trust was given the right to declare its property inalienable, so ensuring that in any subsequent dispute it can appeal directly to parliament.

As it works towards its dual aims of conserving areas of attractive countryside and encouraging greater public access (not easy to reconcile in this age of mass tourism), the Trust provides an excellent service for walkers by creating new concessionary paths and waymarked trails, maintaining stiles and footbridges and combating the ever-increasing problem of footpath erosion.

For details of membership, contact the National Trust at the address on page 95.

 ## The Ramblers

No organisation works more actively to protect and extend the rights and interests of walkers in the countryside than the Ramblers. Its aims are clear: to foster a greater knowledge, love and care of the countryside; to assist in the protection and enhancement of public rights of way and areas of natural beauty; to work for greater public access to the countryside; and to encourage more people to take up rambling as a healthy, recreational leisure activity.

It was founded in 1935 when, following the setting up of a National Council of Ramblers' Federation in 1931, a number of federations in London, Manchester, the Midlands and elsewhere came together to create a more effective pressure group, to deal with such problems as the disappearance or obstruction of footpaths, the prevention of access to open mountain and moorland, and increasing hostility from landowners. This was the era of the mass trespasses, when there were sometimes violent confrontations between ramblers and gamekeepers, especially on the moorlands of the Peak District.

Since then the Ramblers has played a

key role in preserving and developing the national footpath network, supporting the creation of national parks and encouraging the designation and waymarking of long-distance routes.

Our freedom of access to the countryside, now enshrined in legislation, is still in its early years and requires constant vigilance. But over and above this there will always be the problem of footpaths being illegally obstructed, disappearing through lack of use, or being extinguished by housing or road construction.

It is to meet such problems and dangers that the Ramblers exists and represents the interests of all walkers. The address to write to for information on the Ramblers and how to become a member is given on page 95.

 ## Walkers and the Law

The *Countryside and Rights of Way Act 2000 (CRoW)* extends the rights of access previously enjoyed by walkers in England and Wales. Implementation of these rights began on 19 September 2004. The Act amends existing legislation and for the first time provides access on foot to certain types of land – defined as mountain, moor, heath, down and registered common land.

Where You Can Go
Rights of Way

Prior to the introduction of *CRoW* walkers could only legally access the countryside along public rights of way. These are either 'footpaths' (for walkers only) or 'bridleways' (for walkers, riders on horseback and pedal cyclists). A third category called 'Byways open to all traffic' (BOATs), is used by motorised vehicles as well as those using non-mechanised transport. Mainly they are green lanes, farm and estate roads, although occasionally they will be found crossing mountainous area.

Rights of way are marked on Ordnance Survey maps. Look for the green broken lines on the Explorer maps, or the red dashed lines on Landranger maps.

The term 'right of way' means exactly what it says. It gives a right of passage over what, for the most part, is private land. Under pre-CRoW legislation walkers were required to keep to the line of the right of way and not stray onto land on either side. If you did inadvertently wander off the right of way, either because of faulty map reading or because the route was not clearly indicated on the ground, you were technically trespassing.

Local authorities have a legal obligation to ensure that rights of way are kept clear and free of obstruction, and are signposted where they leave metalled roads. The duty of local authorities to install signposts extends to the placing of signs along a path or way, but only where the authority considers it necessary to have a signpost or waymark to assist persons unfamiliar with the locality.

The New Access Rights
Access Land

As well as being able to walk on existing rights of way, under the new legislation you now have access to large areas of open land. You can of course continue to use rights of way footpaths to cross this land, but the main difference is that you can now lawfully leave the path and wander at will, but only in areas designated as access land.

Where to Walk

Areas now covered by the new access rights – Access Land – are shown on Ordnance Survey Explorer maps by a light yellow tint surrounded by a pale orange border. New orange coloured 'i' symbols on the maps will show the location of permanent access information boards installed by the access authorities.

Restrictions

The right to walk on access land may lawfully be restricted by landowners. Landowners can, for any reason, restrict access for up to 28 days in any year. They cannot however close the land:

- on bank holidays;
- for more than four Saturdays and Sundays in a year;

Countryside Access Charter

Your rights of way are:

- public footpaths – on foot only. Sometimes waymarked in yellow
- bridleways – on foot, horseback and pedal cycle. Sometimes waymarked in blue
- byways (usually old roads), most 'roads used as public paths' and, of course, public roads – all traffic has the right of way

Use maps, signs and waymarks to check rights of way. Ordnance Survey Explorer and Landranger maps show most public rights of way

On rights of way you can:

- take a pram, pushchair or wheelchair if practicable
- take a dog (on a lead or under close control)
- take a short route round an illegal obstruction or remove it sufficiently to get past

You have a right to go for recreation to:

- public parks and open spaces – on foot
- most commons near older towns and cities – on foot and sometimes on horseback
- private land where the owner has a formal agreement with the local authority

In addition you can use the following by local or established custom or consent, but ask for advice if you are unsure:

- many areas of open country, such as moorland, fell and coastal areas, especially those in the care of the National Trust, and some commons
- some woods and forests, especially those owned by the Forestry Commission
- country parks and picnic sites
- most beaches
- canal towpaths
- some private paths and tracks Consent sometimes extends to horse-riding and cycling

For your information:

- county councils and London boroughs maintain and record rights of way, and register commons
- obstructions, dangerous animals, harassment and misleading signs on rights of way are illegal and you should report them to the county council
- paths across fields can be ploughed, but must normally be reinstated within two weeks
- landowners can require you to leave land to which you have no right of access
- motor vehicles are normally permitted only on roads, byways and some 'roads used as public paths'

- on any Saturday from 1 June to 11 August; or
- on any Sunday from 1 June to the end of September.

They have to provide local authorities with five working days' notice before the date of closure unless the land involved is an area of less than five hectares or the closure is for less than four hours. In these cases landowners only need to provide two hours' notice.

Whatever restrictions are put into place on access land they have no effect on existing rights of way, and you can continue to walk on them.

Dogs

Dogs can be taken on access land, but must be kept on leads of two metres or less between 1 March and 31 July, and at all times where they are near livestock. In addition landowners may impose a ban on all dogs from fields where lambing takes place for up to six weeks in any year. Dogs may be banned from moorland used for grouse shooting and breeding for up to five years.

In the main, walkers following the routes in this book will continue to follow existing rights of way, but a knowledge and understanding of the law as it affects walkers, plus the ability to distinguish access land marked on the maps, will enable anyone who wishes to depart from paths that cross access land either to take a shortcut, to enjoy a view or to explore.

General Obstructions

Obstructions can sometimes cause a problem on a walk and the most common of these is where the path across a field has been ploughed over. It is legal for a farmer to plough up a path provided that it is restored within two weeks. This does not always happen and you are faced with the dilemma of following the line of the path, even if this means treading on crops, or walking round the edge of the field. Although the later course of action seems the most sensible, it does mean that you would be trespassing.

Other obstructions can vary from overhanging vegetation to wire fences across the path, locked gates or even a cattle feeder on the path.

Use common sense. If you can get round the obstruction without causing damage, do so. Otherwise only remove as much of the obstruction as is necessary to secure passage.

If the right of way is blocked and cannot be followed, there is a long-standing view that in such circumstances there is a right to deviate, but this cannot wholly be relied on. Although it is accepted in law that highways (and that includes rights of way) are for the public service, and if the usual track is impassable, it is for the general good that people should be entitled to pass into another line. However, this should not be taken as indicating a right to deviate whenever a way becomes impassable. If in doubt, retreat.

Report obstructions to the local authority and/or the Ramblers.

 ## Global Positioning System (GPS)

What is GPS?

GPS is a worldwide radio navigation system that uses a network of 24 satellites and receivers, usually hand-held, to calculate positions. By measuring the time it takes a signal to reach the receiver, the distance from the satellite can be estimated. Repeat this with several satellites and the receiver

can then use triangulation to establish the position of the receiver.

How to use GPS with Ordnance Survey mapping

Each of the walks in this book includes GPS co-ordinate data that reflects the walk position points on Ordnance Survey maps.

GPS and OS maps use different models for the earth and co-ordinate systems, so when you are trying to relate your GPS position to features on the map the two will differ slightly. This is especially the case with height, as the model that relates the GPS global co-ordinate system to height above sea level is very poor.

When using GPS with OS mapping, some distortion – up to 16ft (5m) – will always be present. Moreover, individual features on maps may have been surveyed only to an accuracy of 23ft (7m) (for 1:25000 scale maps), while other features, e.g. boulders, are usually only shown schematically.

In practice, this should not cause undue difficulty, as you will be near enough to your objective to be able to spot it.

How to use the GPS data in this book

There are various ways you can use the GPS data in this book.

1. Follow the route description while checking your position on your receiver when you are approaching a position point.

2. You can also use the positioning information on your receiver to verify where you are on the map.

3. Alternatively, you can use some of the proprietary software that is available. At the simple end there is inexpensive software, which lets you input the walk positions (waypoints), download them to the gps unit and then use them to assist your navigation on the walks.

At the upper end of the market Ordnance Survey maps are available in electronic form. Most come with software that enables you to enter your walking route onto the map, download it to your gps unit and use it, alongside the route description, to follow the route.

Safety on the Hills

The hills, mountains and moorlands of Britain, though of modest height compared with those in many other countries, need to be treated with respect. Friendly and inviting in good weather, they can quickly be transformed into wet, misty, windswept and potentially dangerous areas of wilderness in bad weather. Even on an outwardly fine and settled summer day, conditions can rapidly deteriorate. In winter, of course, the weather can be even more erratic and the hours of daylight are much shorter.

Therefore it is advisable to always take both warm and waterproof clothing, sufficient nourishing food, a hot drink, first-aid kit, torch and whistle. Wear suitable footwear, such as strong walking boots or shoes that give a good grip over rocky terrain and on slippery slopes. Try to obtain a local weather forecast and bear it in mind before you start. Do not be afraid to abandon your proposed route and return to your starting point in the event of a sudden and unexpected deterioration in the weather. Do not go alone. Allow enough time to finish the walk well before nightfall.

Most of the walks described in this book do not venture into remote wilderness areas and will be safe to do, given due care and respect, at any time of year in all but the most unreasonable weather. Indeed, a crisp, fine winter day often provides perfect walking conditions, with firm ground underfoot and a clarity that is not possible to achieve in the other seasons of the year. A few walks, however, are suitable only for reasonably fit and experienced hill-walkers able to use a compass and should definitely not be tackled by anyone else during the winter months or in bad weather, especially high winds and mist. These are indicated in the general description that precedes each of the walks.

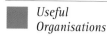

Useful Organisations

Campaign to Protect Rural England
5-11 Lavington Street, London SE1 0NZ
Tel. 020 7981 2800
www.cpre.org.uk

Forestry Commission
Yorkshire and North East of England regional office
Room G34, Foss House,
Kings Pool,
1-2 Peasholme Green,
York, YO1 7PX
Tel. 0300 067 4900
www.forestry.gov.uk

Long Distance Walkers' Association
www.ldwa.org.uk

National Trust
Membership and general enquiries:
Tel. 0344 8001895
North East Regional Office:
Holy Jesus Hospital, City Road,
Newcastle-upon-Tyne NE1 2AS
Tel: 0191 2558600
www.nationaltrust.org.uk

Natural England
North East regional office
Lancaster House, Hampshire Court,
Newcastle upon Tyne,
NE4 7YH
Tel. 0300 060 3900
www.gov.uk/government/organisations/natural-england

North Pennines AONB Partnership
Weardale Business Centre,
Old-Coop Building,
1 Martin Street
Stanhope, County
Durham
DL13 2UY
Tel. 01388 528801
www.northpennines.org.uk

Ordnance Survey
Tel. 03456 05 05 05
www.ordnancesurvey.co.uk

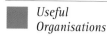

Ramblers
2nd Floor, Camelford House,
87–90 Albert Embankment,
London SE1 7TW
Tel. 020 7339 8500
www.ramblers.org.uk

Rights of Way
Co. Durham
Tel. 03000 265342
www.durham.gov.uk/prow
Cumbria
Tel. 03003 032992
www.cumbria.gov.uk

Tourist information:
www.thisisdurham.com

*Tourist information centres (*not open
all year):*
*Alston: 01434 382244
Appleby-in-Westmorland: 017683 51177
*Brampton: 016977 3433
Darlington: 01325 388666
Durham and Dales: 03000 262626
Gateshead: 0191 433 8420
Kirkby Stephen: 017683 71199
Middleton-in-Teesdale: 01833 641001
South Shields: 0191 424 7788
Sunderland: 0191 561 8494

Youth Hostels Association
Trevelyan House, Dimple Road,
Matlock, Derbyshire DE4 3YH
Tel. 01629 592700
www.yha.org.uk

Weather forecasts:
www.metoffice.gov.uk

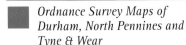
Ordnance Survey Maps of Durham, North Pennines and Tyne & Wear

The area of *Durham, North Pennines and Tyne & Wear* is covered by Ordnance Survey 1:50 000 (1¼ inches to 1 mile or 2cm to 1km) scale Landranger map sheets 86, 87, 88, 90, 91, 92, 93, 94. These all-purpose maps are packed with information to help you explore the area and show viewpoints, picnic sites, places of interest and caravan and camping sites.

To examine the area in more detail and especially if you are planning walks, Ordnance Survey Explorer maps at 1:25 000 (2½ inches to 1 mile or 4cm to 1km) scale are ideal:

304 (Darlington & Richmond)
305 (Bishop Auckland)
306 (Middlesbrough & Hartlepool)
307 (Consett & Derwent Reservoir)
308 (Durham & Sunderland)
315 (Carlisle)
316 (Newcastle upon Tyne)
OL5 (The English Lakes – North-eastern area)
OL19 (Howgill Fells & Upper Eden Valley)
OL30 (Yorkshire Dales – Northern & Central areas)
OL31 (North Pennines – Teesdale & Weardale)
OL43 (Hadrian's Wall – Haltwhistle & Hexham)

Ordnance Survey maps and guides are available from most booksellers, stationers and newsagents.

Further Information

Ordnance Survey

Pathfinder® Guides | Britain's best-loved walking guides